Cover Image By Tricia Bohannan, Student

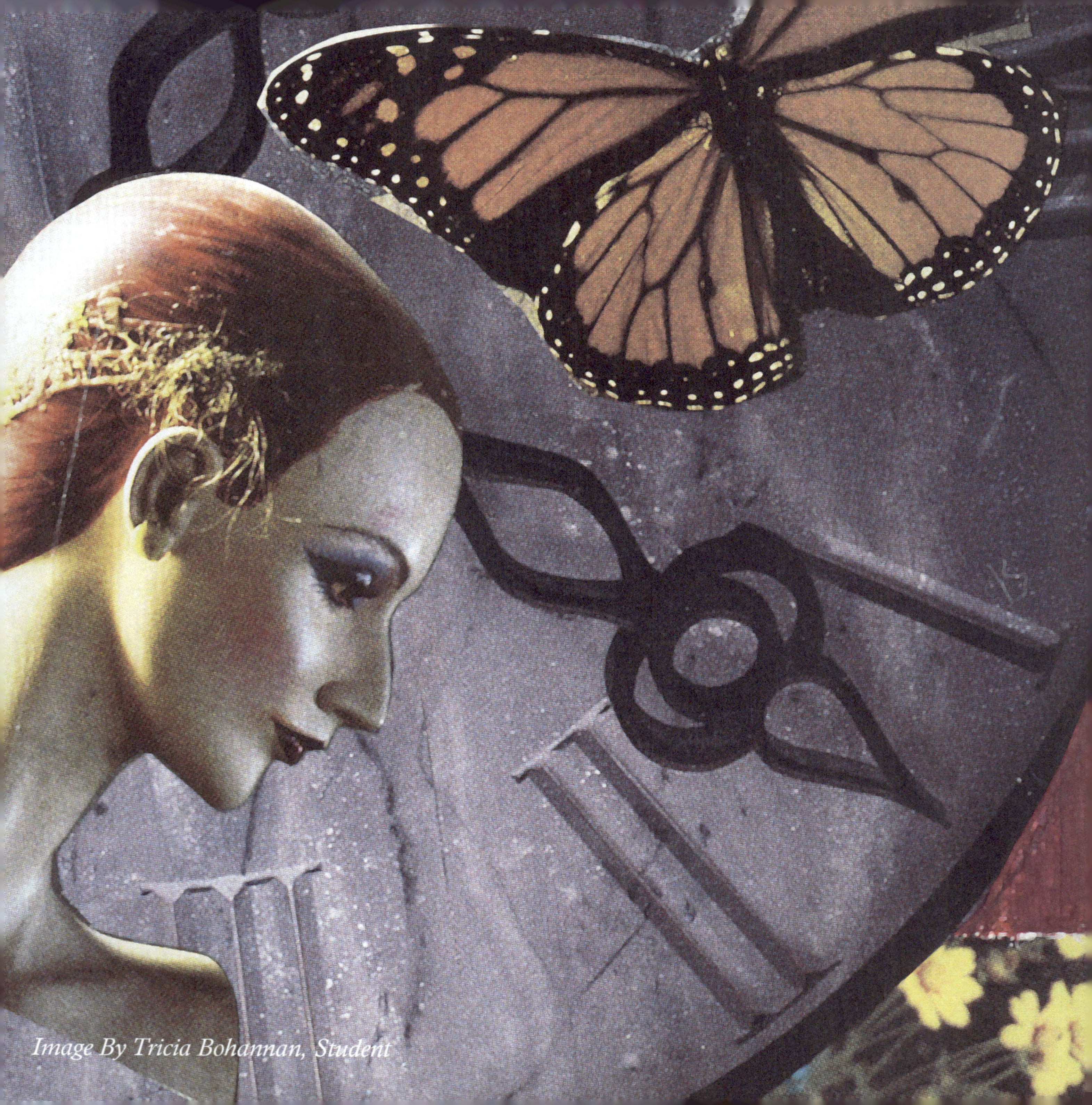

Image By Tricia Bohannan, Student

Artist Postcards

Creating and Communicating Through The Arts

Sarah Cress

Lulu.com number 3053595

ISBN 978-0-578-02623-7

Paperback edition published in 2008 by Sarah Cress, Chicago, Illinois

Graphic design
Sarah Cress, Chicago, Illinois

Printed and bound by Lulu.com

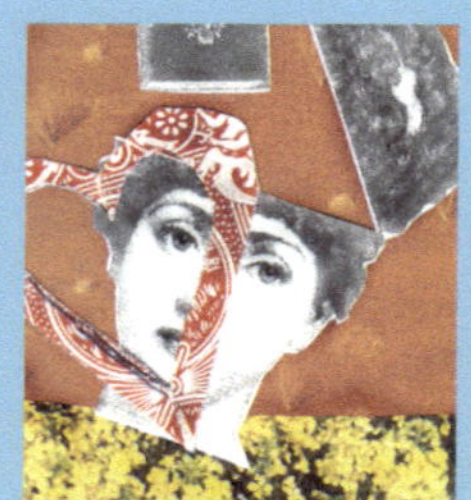

Sarah Cress
Chicago, Illlinois
www.sarahcress.com
sarahcress@gmail.com

Image to Right By Tricia Bohannan, Student

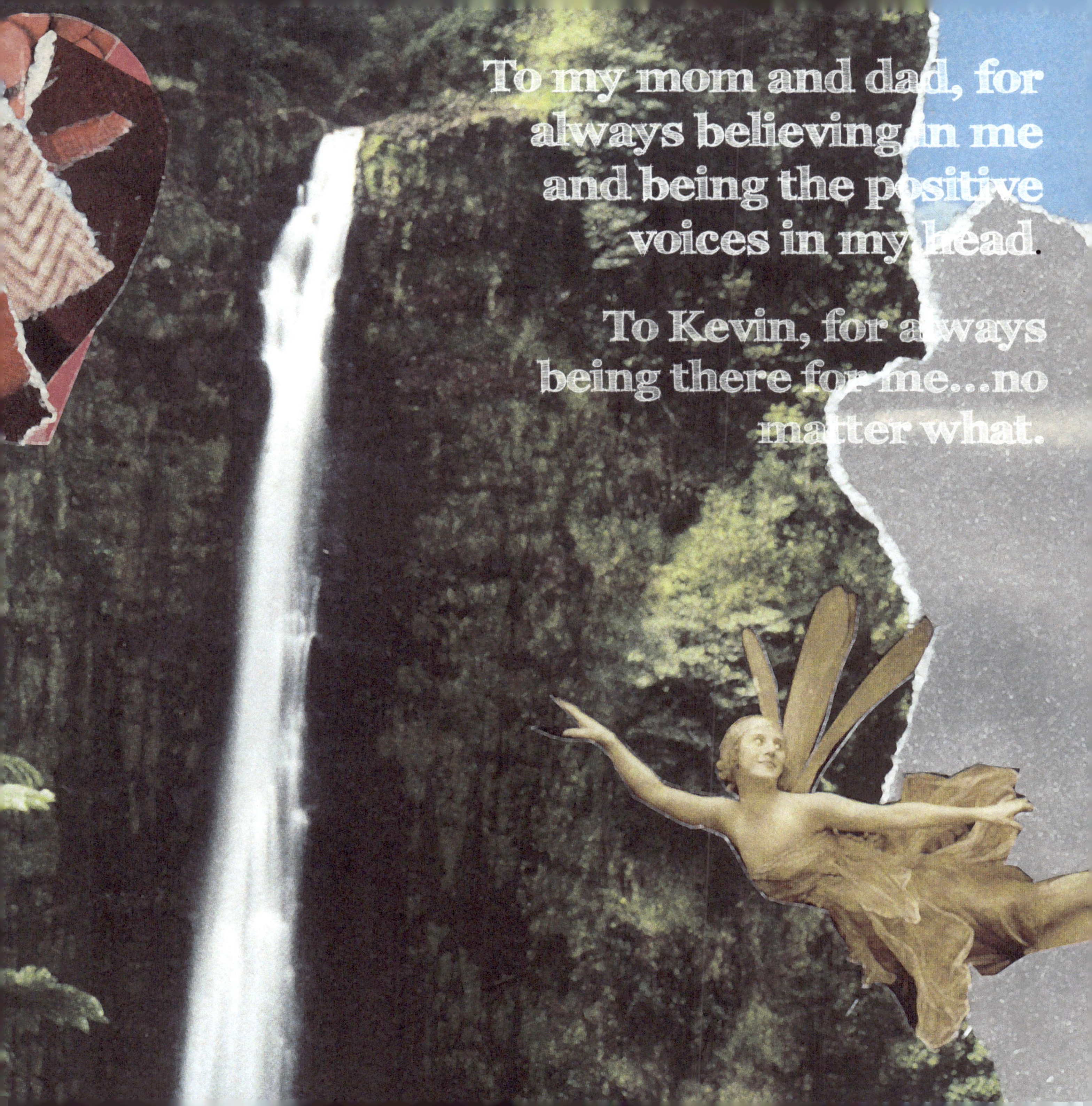
To my mom and dad, for always believing in me and being the positive voices in my head.
To Kevin, for always being there for me...no matter what.

Contents

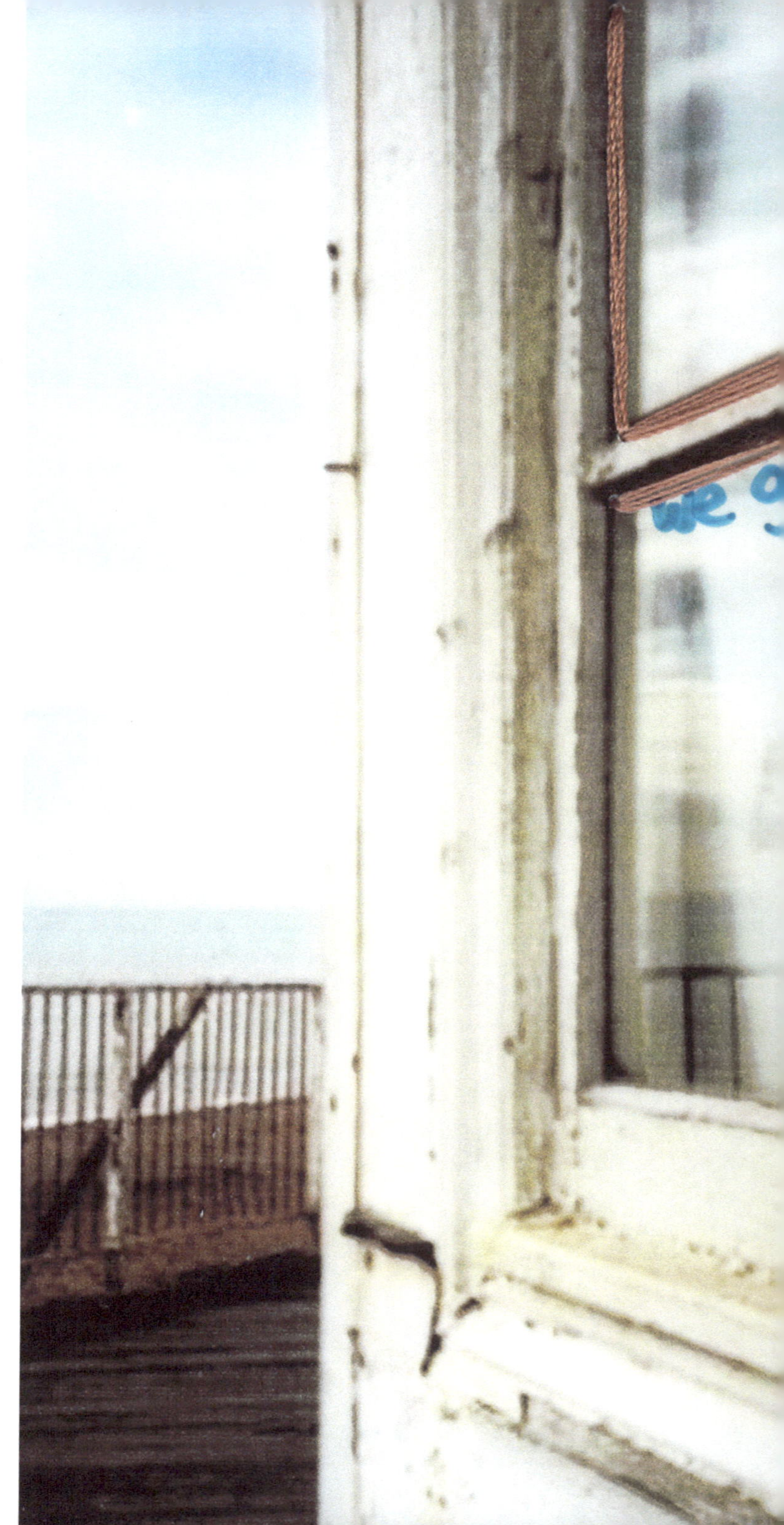

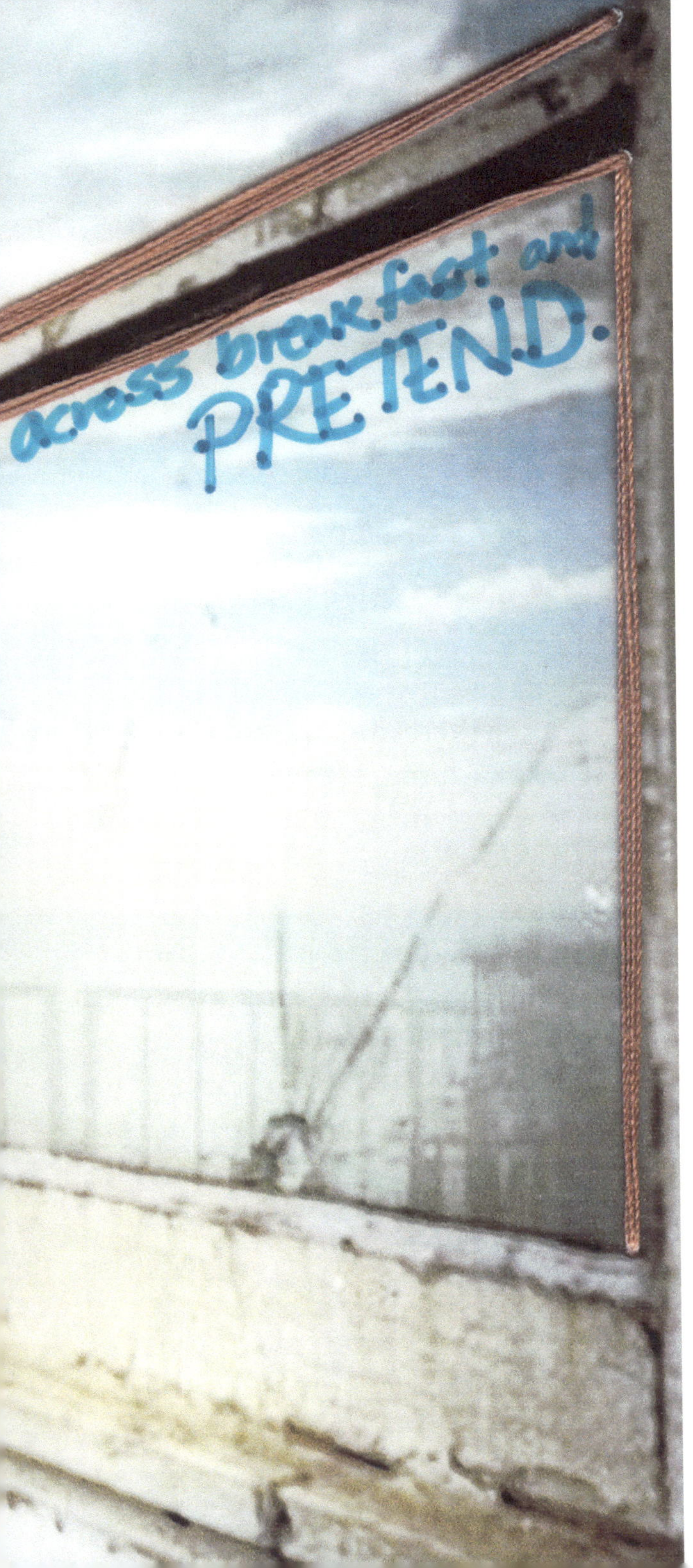

Postcard By Sarah Chambers, Student

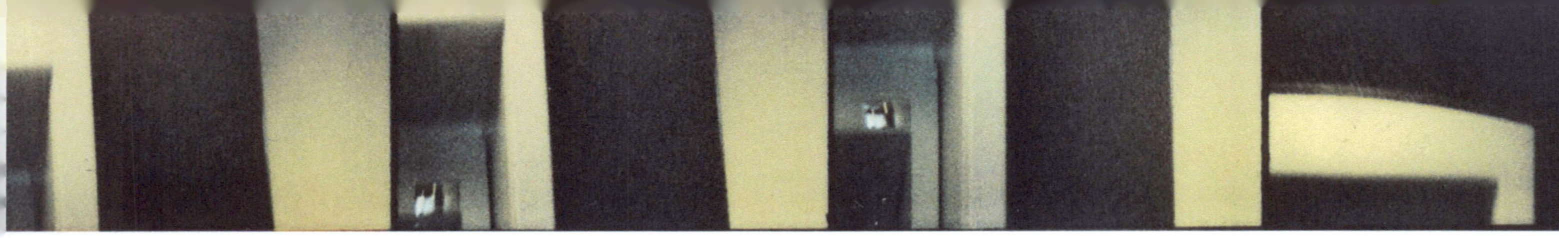

Introduction...

It was during the beginning of my second year of teaching high school photography, when students were talking incessantly about such websites as MySpace© and Facebook©, that I decided it was crucial I address my students' current means of communication. I held an informal discussion with my students requesting information in regards to their experiences communicating with their peers online. I found through their commentary that online chatting and messaging is a part of their daily existence. In many cases, students will spend hours in front of the computer screen typing messages and comments and uploading images and videos through these interactive sites. I asked the students how often they send letters or postcards in the mail. Unsurprisingly, few had many experiences with the postal service. In a world in which our youth are bred to craze immediate satisfaction, the postal service comes up short in the venue of communication.

After thinking about my students' crazed obsession for immediate online satisfaction, I thought about ways of slowing down their speed-based approach to communicating with the world. Thinking back to my grade school years and my experiences writing various pen-pals over the course of my childhood, I decided to incorporate the idea of Artist Postcards into their learning. A variation of artist trading cards, my students would create small art pieces that they would then address to a pen-pal of their own on the back. The students would entertain a variety of artistic media and processes to create their theme-based correspondence.

I introduced the Artist Postcard project to my advanced photography students and assigned them pen-pals arranged through my co-operating mentor from high school student teaching. My Streamwood, Illinois based students were now engulfed in a communication trail with students from Urbana, Illinois.

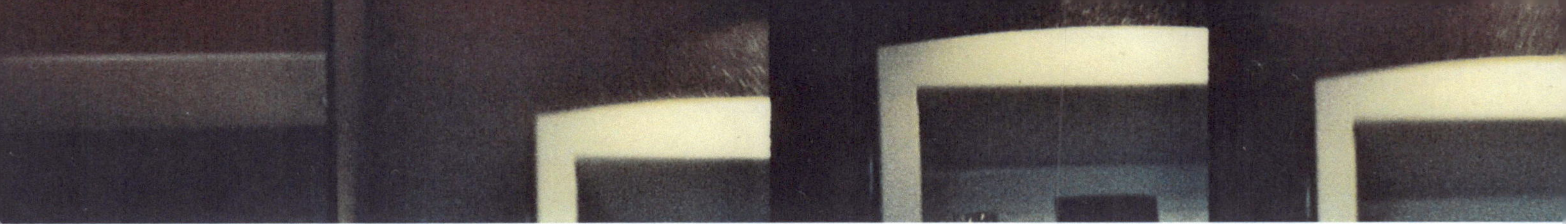

During the art making process students created works that utilized their basic knowledge of photographic processes, in addition to collage, montage and alternative processes. The students would brainstorm and create imagery based on a variety of themes. Once the students completed each postcard, they would take part in a peer critique to gauge quality and interest of each piece.

With each postcard session, the students learned about one another through their artistic creations, in addition to their written word. With each postcard batch sent, my students would wait anxiously for their pen-pals to reply. While waiting for their cards to arrive many students went online to have discussions with their pen-pals through Myspace© and Facebook©. The students were eager to learn more about their southern counterparts and the lives that they lived. Although online discussions became more frequent among the students, nothing surpassed the experience of holding the unique artwork they received in the mail. The students were excited with each batch to see what the others had created just for them.

At the end of their year-long experience, my students put together a collaborative three-dimensional postcard that they sent to the Urbana class. The students brought in small objects that represented something of importance in their life, and then assembled them in a shadow box for display. This concluding collaboration was a meaningful way for my students to bring closure to the experience. Several of my students have expressed to me that they intend on continuing their communication with their pen-pals through online correspondence and/or art sharing.

The purpose of this lesson was manifold. Not only did I want to encourage the continued artistic development and creativity of my students, but I also wanted to engage them in writing and artistic critique. Upon completion of this year-long project, I discovered that my students learned more than I had anticipated. My students learned about themselves, the process of communication, and the power of the visual image.

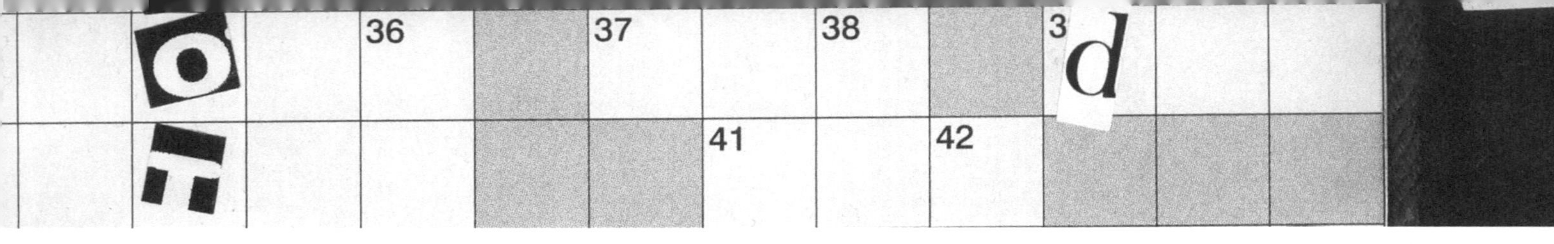

Lesson Plan...

Aim/Goal of the Curriculum: The students will begin to focus upon photography as a visual and meaningful way of expressing oneself in the world today. The students will take their current knowledge of basic artistic skills and manipulate those techniques to create outcomes that reflect a style of their very own. In order to discover their own style, the students must experiment with a variety of materials. By the end of the school term the students should be able to create a variety of works that demonstrate the breadth of knowledge they have gained throughout this course. The students will also understand the power of the visual as a valuable communication tool.

Fine Arts Goals Met By the Objectives: (Illinois) 25.A.4, 25.B.4, 26.B.4e, 26.B.4d, 27.A.4b, 27.B.4b

Objectives:

Creative/Productive Objective: The students will participate in a year-long collaboration with a distant high school. Each student will be assigned one to two students in which they will communicate through their own artistic creations. The students will create a five inch by seven inch Artist Postcard for each of their pen-pals. The students will create the visual side of their cards experimenting with a variety of themes and photographic processes. The students will address the back of their postcards to their pen-pals, and begin a commentary that will continue with each mailing. Once the students complete their Artist Postcards the teacher will send them to the high school to which they are addressed.

Multicultural/Historical Objective: The students will begin their extensive experience with Artist Postcards by discussing the relevancy of the postcard icon and its role in society. The students will compare postcards to the other means of communication that they use on a regular basis. The students will look at a variety of historical and contemporary postcards and discuss their artistic and compositional characteristics. The students will use their understanding of the postcard as a communicative tool to enhance their own designs.

Affective/Expressive Objective: While creating their Artist Postcards the students will experience a variety of media and processes. Through demonstration of these processes, the students will be expected to create Artist Postcards that are creative, aesthetically appealing and sensitive to their viewers. With each mailing, the students will not only respond to their pen-pals via text, but through their artistic creations as well.

Concepts/Vocabulary:

Creative/Productive Concepts:

Positive space – the compositional space that is inhabited by the primary subject matter of the work.

Negative space – the compositional space surrounding the primary subject matter.

Composition – the act of combining parts or elements to form a whole.

Layout - an arrangement or plan.

Leading Lines – lines that direct the attention of the viewer

Framing – a border or case for enclosing a picture.

Contrast - the contrast is the degree of difference between the dark and the light areas of a scene or photograph. High contrast photographs are a result of high contrast lighting, where there are sharp differences in the dark and light, and less in between.

Montage – the technique of combining in a single composition elements from a variety of sources.

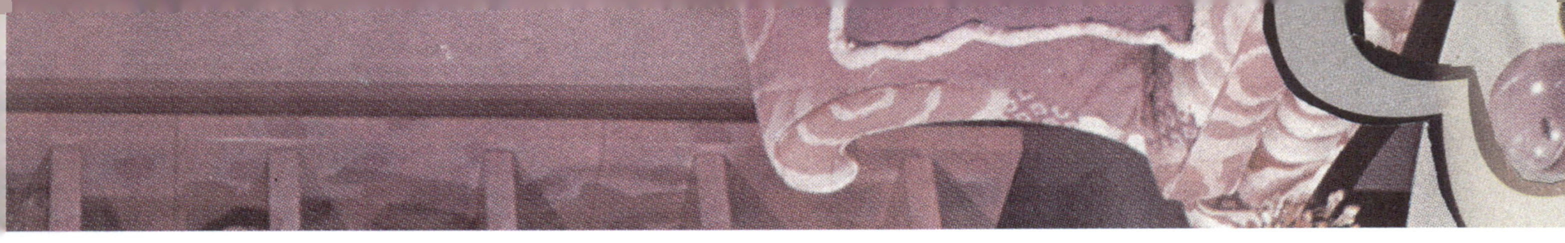

Collage – a technique of art making in which various materials and images are combined on one single surface.
Still Image – a photograph depicting still life.
Scene – a photograph depicting a place where some action or event occurs.
Alternative Processes – photographic processes that involve working outside of the darkroom or computer lab.
Cyanotype – a photographic process that involves the mixing of Ferric Ammonium Citrate and Potassium Ferricyanide to create a light sensitive surface.
Vandyke Brown – a photographic process that involves the mixing of Ferric Ammonium Citrate, Tartaric Acid and Silver Nitrate to create a light sensitive surface.
Contact Print – in the darkroom the act of exposing a piece of light sensitive material by placing an image or object on top of it underneath the enlarger.
Portrait – an image representing the liking of an individual.
Wide Angle – in photography, the act of using a lens with a wide angle of viewing.

Multicultural/Historical Concepts:
Postcards – an image that has space for a message, address and stamp on the back which can be mailed
Visual Media – any piece of media that incorporates the power of the visual image: billboards, magazines, newspapers, movie posters, commercials, fliers, etc.
Visual Culture – the elements of culture that invade the domain of the visual. Visual media makes up our visual culture.
Mail – the process of sending written communications to others via mail.
Communication – the means in which we share thoughts, ideas and opinions. This can be achieved through spoken word, written text, artistic creation, etc.
Iconography – a collection of visual imagery that represents a particular subject matter.
Protest – the act of addressing an issue that you feel is unfair or unjust.
Controversial – an issue that is extremely questionable or debatable.

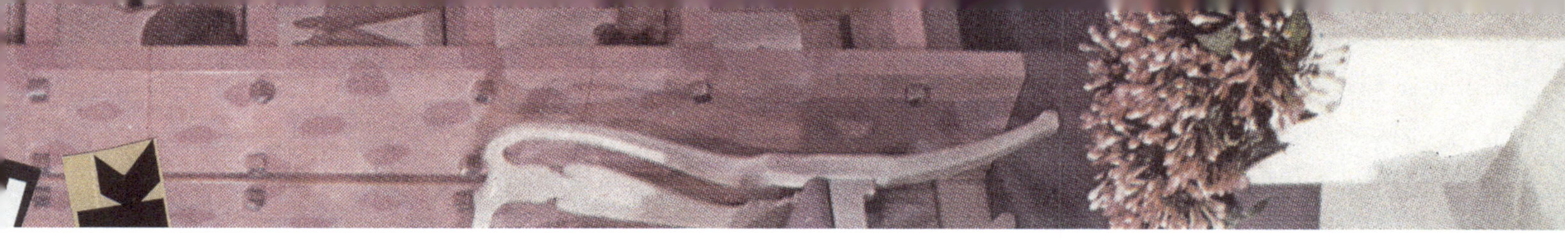

Affective/Expressive Concepts:
Context – The circumstances that surround a particular event, situation, etc.
Individualism – Having the ability to express one's individual beliefs and ideas.
Interpretation – An explanation of the meaning of another's artistic or creative work.
Visual Literacy – Comprehension of the visual communication expressed by a piece of artwork.
Characteristics – The unique elements that make up a particular individual.
Reflection – The process of observing and considering the influence of a person, place or thing on another individual.

Materials:

Visual Exemplars:
Historical and contemporary postcards
Teacher examples of postcards
Student examples of postcards
Video commentary of student experiences

Teacher Materials:

Digital Postcards:
Digital camera
Adobe Photoshop
Cardstock
Tripod
Printer
Photographic printer paper
Printer ink

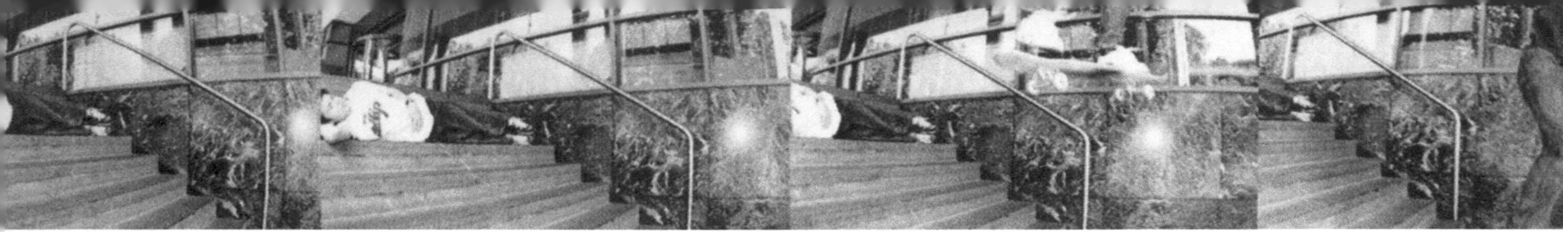

Darkroom Produced Postcards:
- 35mm SLR Camera
- 35mm black and white film and color film
- Medium format camera
- Medium format black and white film
- Darkroom enlarger and accessories
- Darkroom chemicals for film and print development
- Light sensitive photographic paper
- Fisheye camera
- Eight lens camera
- Tripod

Alternative Process Postcards:
- Watercolor paper
- Sponge brushes
- Tongs
- Plastic gloves
- Beakers
- Weight
- Cyanotype chemical mixture
- Van Dyke Brown chemical mixture
- Paper trimmer or scissors
- Contact glass

Montage/Collage Postcards:
- Decorative paper
- Magazines
- Newspapers
- Adhesive
- Found objects

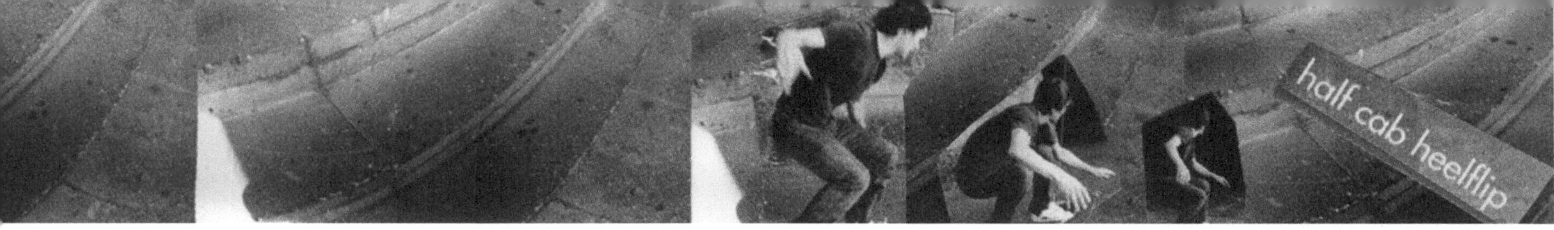

Student Materials:

Digital Postcards:
- Cardstock
- Photographic printer paper

Darkroom Produced Postcards:
- 35mm black and white film
- 35mm color film
- Medium format black and white film
- Light sensitive photographic paper

Alternative Process Postcards:
- Watercolor paper
- Cyanotype chemical mixture
- Vandyke brown chemical mixture

Montage/Collage Postcards:
- Decorative paper
- Magazines
- Newspapers
- Found objects

Motivation: The students will begin their exploration into the world of Artist Postcards with a discussion of the role of postcards in today's society. They will compare and contrast the characteristics of the postcard with other current and past means of communication.

Discussion Questions:
- What is the role of the postcard?
- What does a postcard represent to you?

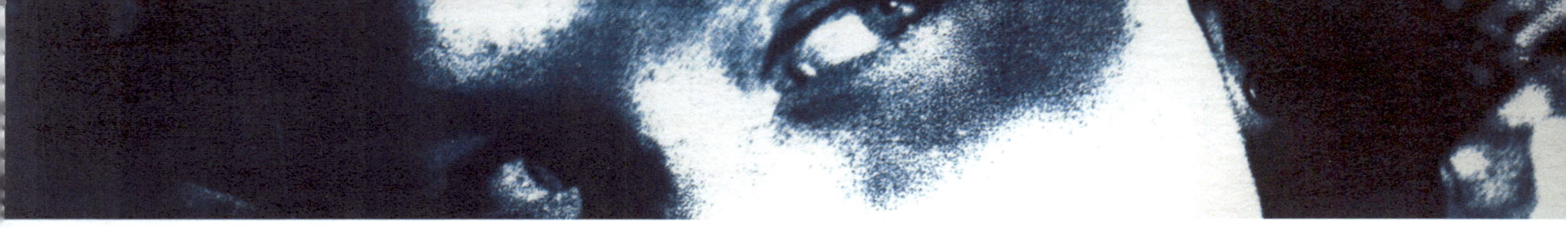

What was the last time you received a postcard?
What images did you see on that postcard?
What message was written on the back of the postcard?
How often do we use postcards today?
What do we use postcards for?
What other means of communication do we use?
How can we compare and contrast these new means of communication to the postcard?
What does our current means of communication say about our broader society?

The students will look at and interpret a variety of teacher and student examples of Artist Postcards.

Discussion Questions:

What are your impressions of the Artist Postcards viewed?
How are these Artist Postcards similar to existing postcards?
How are these Artist Postcards different from existing postcards?
What Artist Postcards stand out to you?
What makes these compositions visually engaging?

The students will then create an Artist Postcard for a family or friend that they have not seen in a while. The students will create a basic collage Artist Postcard depicting some of the events in their life that have occurred since the last meeting of their pen-pal.

Student Reflections and Closure:

Once the students complete each postcard, they will answer the following questions in reflection of their process:

What did you learn during this artistic experience?

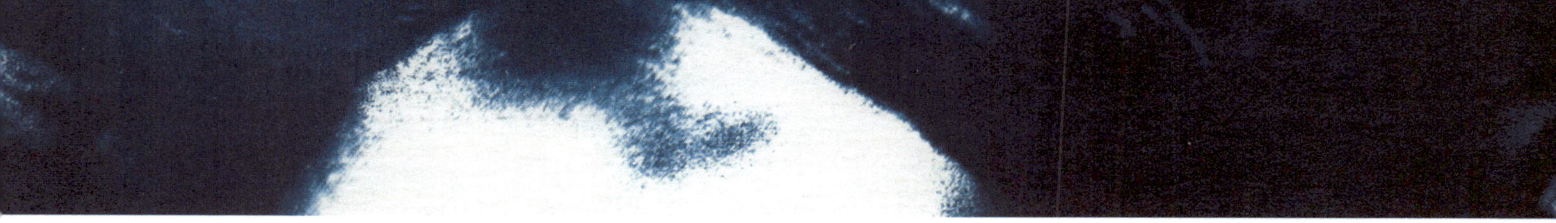

What did you intend to accomplish during the completion of your composition?
Were you successful in this? Why or why not?
If you were to do this postcard again, what would you do differently?
How do you think the recipient of your work will interpret your imagery?
What expectations do you have for your recipient in return?

After the completion of all ten postcards, the students will reflect upon their overall experiences communicating with a peer through the creation of artwork. The students will answer the following questions as a class:

What did you learn during this artistic experience?
Did you enjoy the practice of exchanging Artist Postcards? Why or why not?
Do you feel that you learned a lot about your pen-pal through postcard exchange? Why or why not?
Do you feel that your pen-pal knows a lot about you?
Do you plan on continuing your correspondence with your pen-pal in the future? In what capacity will you continue this correspondence?
What did you learn about yourself as an artist during this experience?

Preparation Time:
Research and gathering of examples: 6 hours
Creating teacher materials: 8 hours
Time prior to each class for preparation: 1 hour
Duration of each class period: 50 minutes

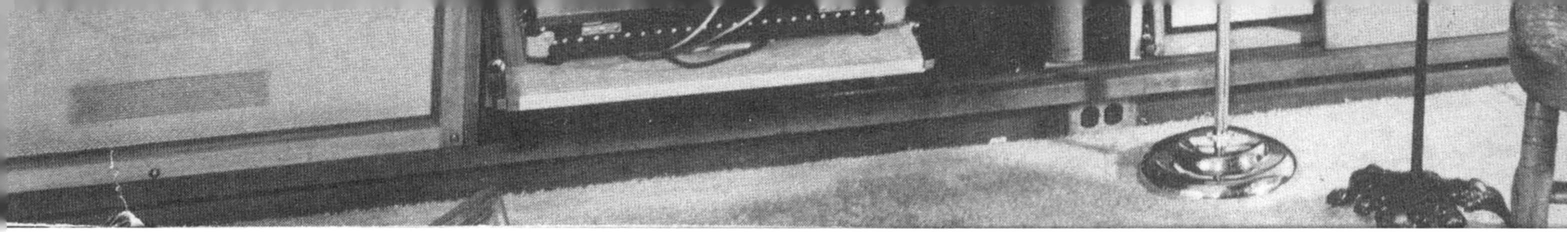

Prompts to Get You Started...

My favorite type of music is...
My favorite musical artist is...
My favorite photographer...
My favorite place to be...
My expectations of the future...
My personal idol...
My favorite memory...
My most embarrassing moment...
My favorite color is...
I feel sad when...
I feel happy when...
This cheers me up...
My personal role model...
What I want to be when I grow up...
If I could go on any vacation without a budget it would be...
When I get home from school, the first thing I do is...
My favorite thing to do on a Saturday...
My family is important to me because...
Where I see myself in ten years...
Where I see myself in twenty years...
If I had my own reality tv show, people would learn this about me...
My favorite movie is...
If I could leave my mark on the world it would be...
I am creating a time capsule of memories. I will include...
My response to worldly affairs...

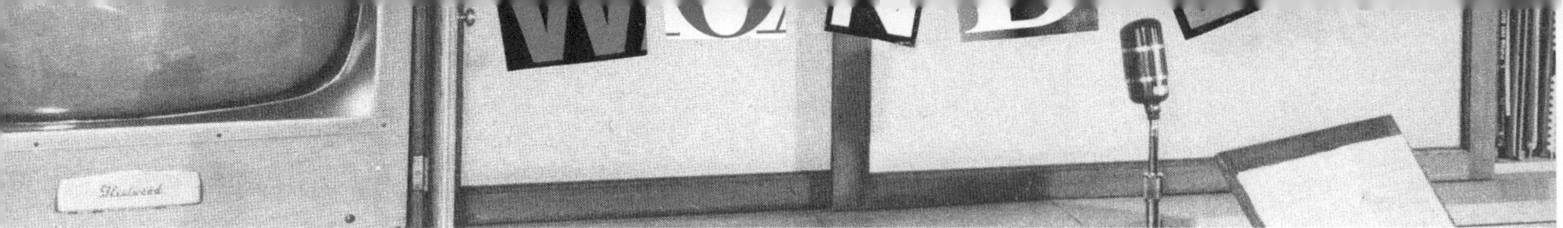

My response to the war…
If I were President of the United States…
If I had a million dollars, I would…
If I could photograph anywhere in the world I would go to…
If I were homeless, life would look like this…
If I were rich, life would look like this…
My favorite foods…
When I look at celebrities I see…
If I were Miss America…
I am most afraid of…
I wish I was ________ right now…
The best part of photography class is…

Individual Postcard Procedures...

Postcard One: Digital Exploration

The students will create an Artist Postcard using their knowledge of the digital image. The students will choose one of the following themes for the focus of their first postcard: emphasis of size, depiction of emotion, false stereotypes. The students will interpret the theme chosen and take one digital photograph for the visual side of their postcard. The students will print their images on cardstock and write an introductory note on the back telling their pen-pal about themselves.

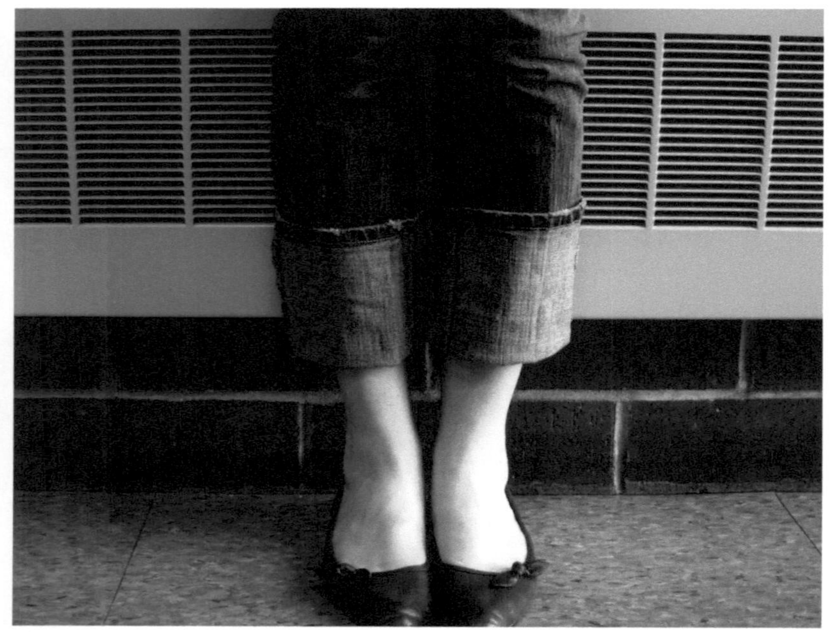

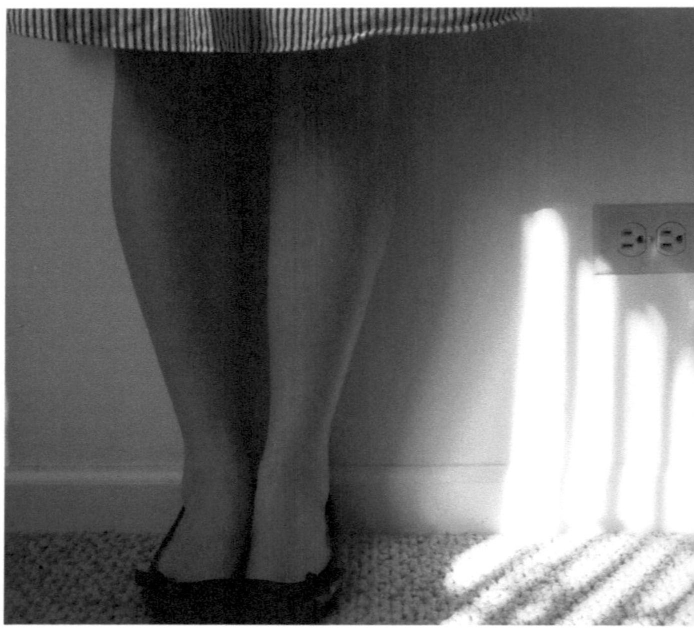

Postcards By Sarah Chambers, Student

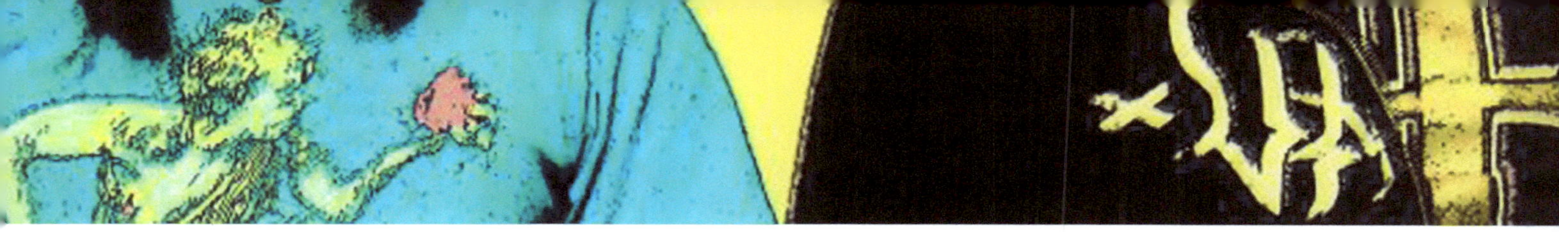

Postcard Two: Digital Manipulation

The students will create an Artist Postcard using their knowledge of the digital image and experiment with various Photoshop tools to create a manipulation. The students will choose one of the following themes for the focus of their postcard: the future, that's delicious, man's impact on the world. After uploading their images to Photoshop, the students may apply their knowledge of any of the following Photoshop techniques to their Artist Postcard design:

- gradients
- adjustment layers and levels
- color variations
- filtration
- digital montage
- textured and translucent overlays
- vignettes
- hand coloring
- cross processing
- silhouettes
- halftones
- panoramas

The students will print their postcards onto cardstock.

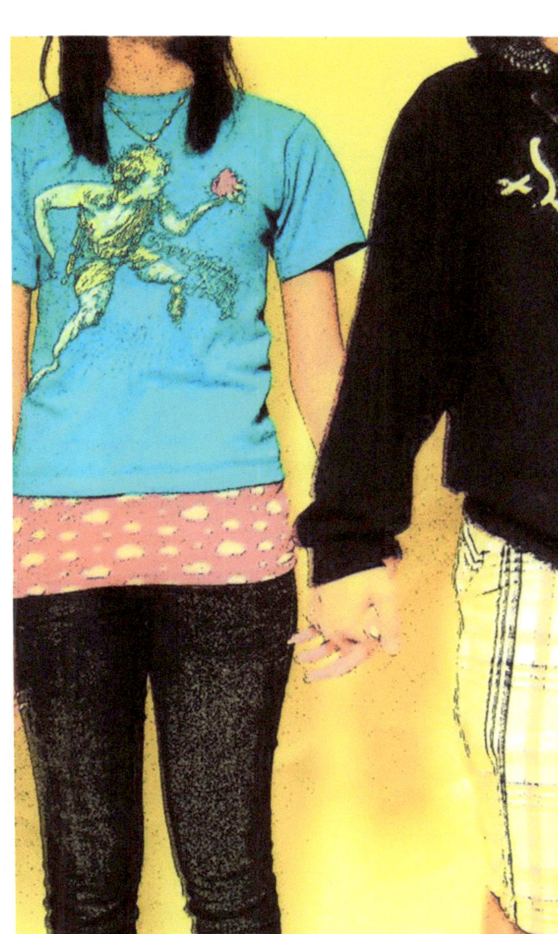

Postcards By Tricia Bohannan, Student

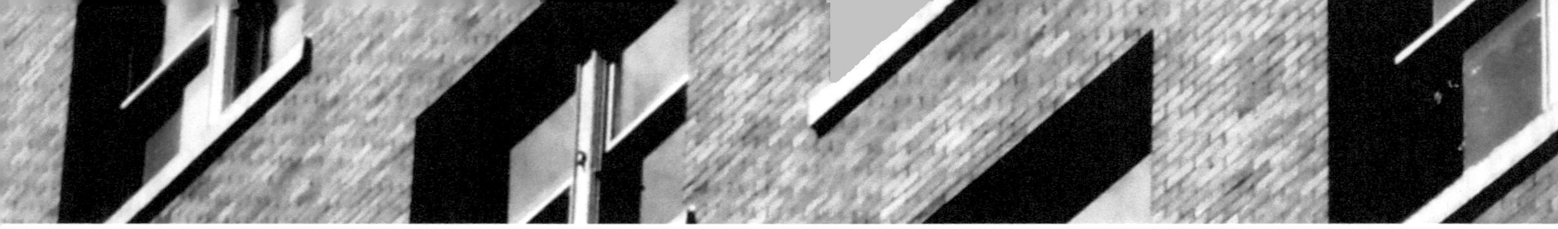

Postcard Three: Darkroom Exposures

The students will create an Artist Postcard using their knowledge of the 35mm negative and the darkroom. The students will create a one image composition that illustrates their interpretation of one of the following themes: geometry geometry geometry, on the move, out of place, wide angles. The students will shoot their compositions using a 35mm SLR camera and develop their film and prints in the darkroom. The students will print their imagery to the size of their Artist Postcards.

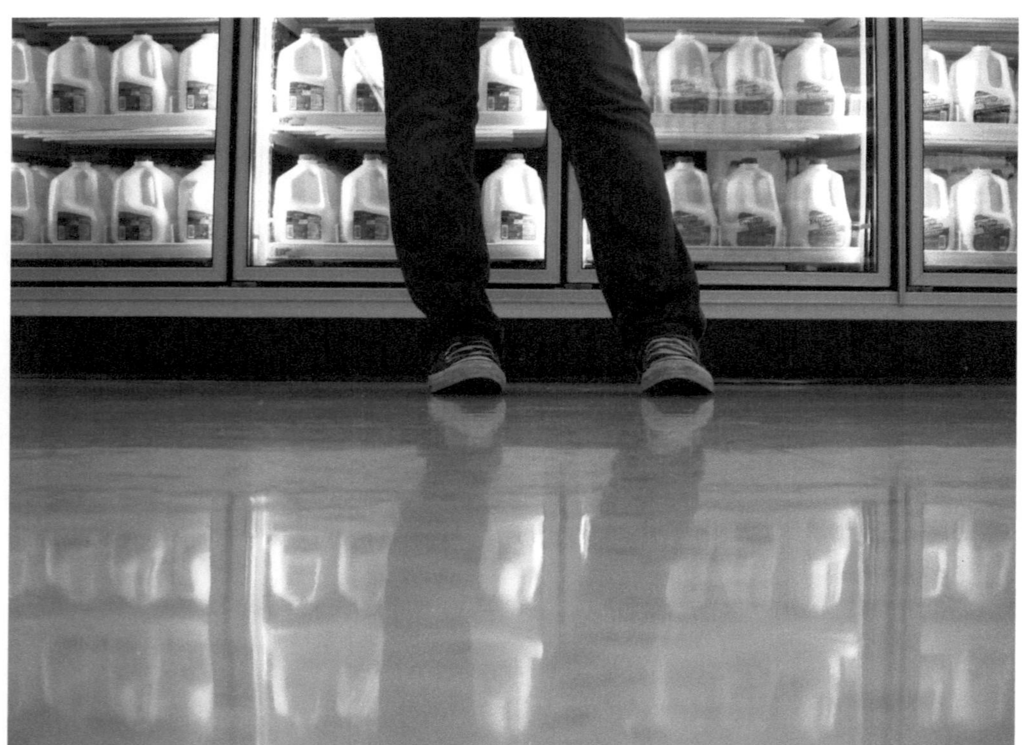

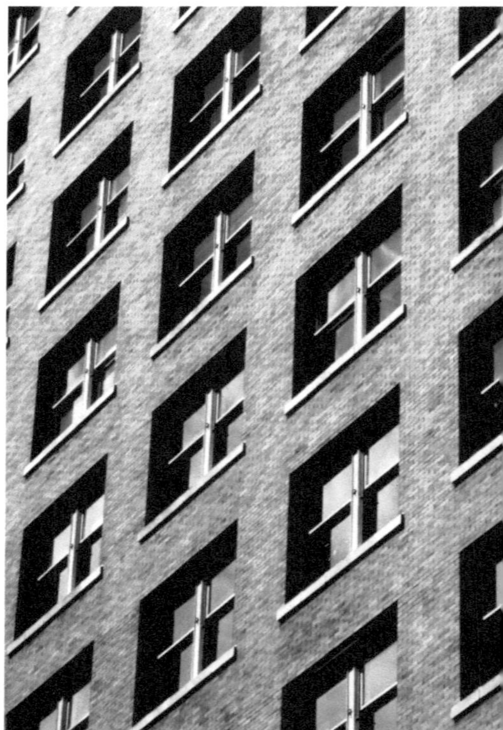

Postcards By Sarah Chambers, Student

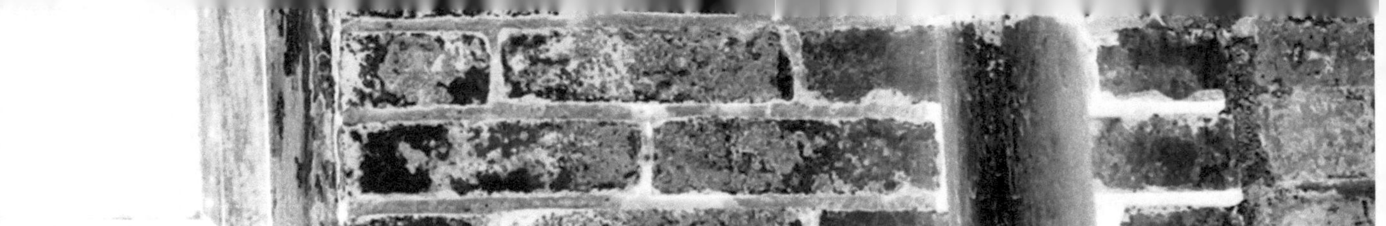

Postcard Four: Darkroom Manipulations

The students will create an Artist Postcard using their knowledge of the 35mm negative and various darkroom manipulations. The students will create a one image composition that illustrates their interpretation of one of the following themes: diptych associations, the world without people, my favorite dream. The students will shoot their compositions using a 35mm SLR camera and develop their film and prints in the darkroom. The students will print their imagery to the size of their Artist Postcards. During the printing process, the students may apply their knowledge of any of the following darkroom manipulations:

- filtration
- screen prints
- contact prints
- vignettes
- developer manipulations
- preliminary exposures
- negative sandwiching
- combination printing
- alternative processes

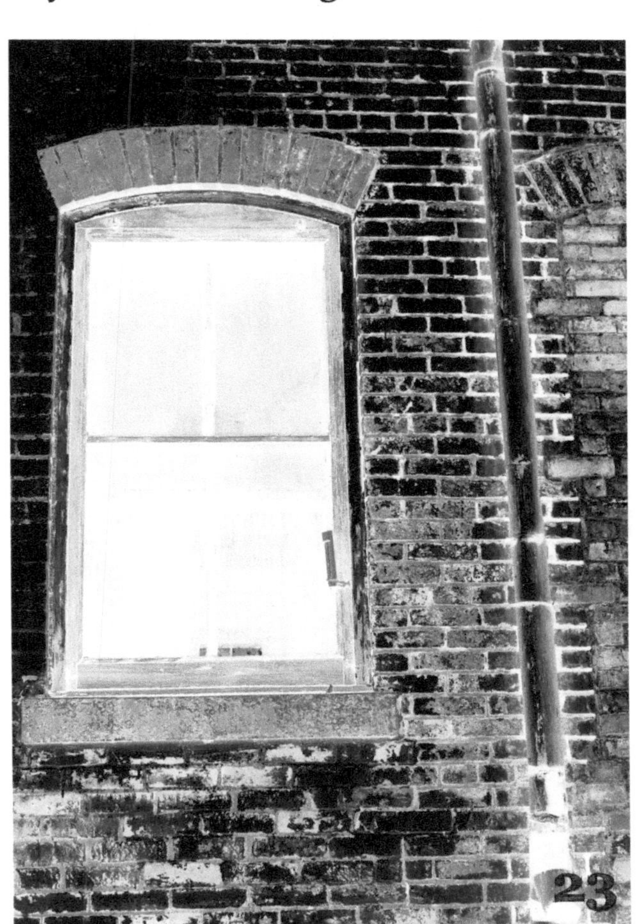

Postcard By Sarah Cress

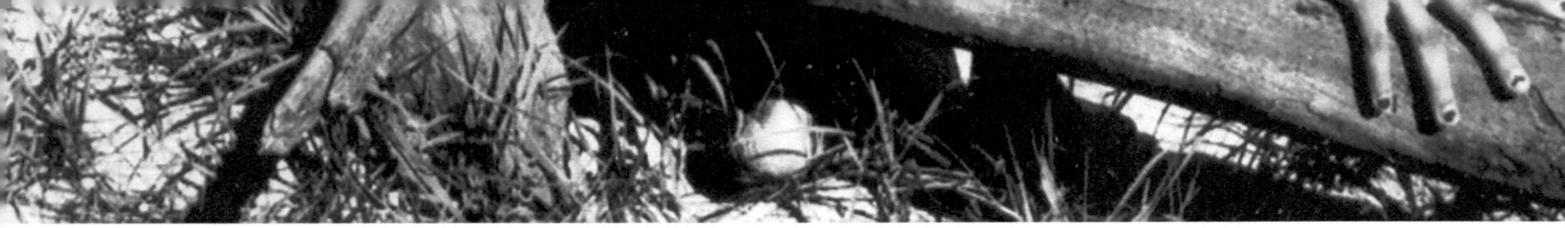

Postcard Five: The Square Perspective

The students will create an Artist Postcard using their knowledge of the medium format negative and the darkroom. The students will shoot a roll of medium format black and white film that focuses on the personal heroes in their life. The students will develop their roll of film in the darkroom and choose their strongest image to create a five inch by five inch print for their Artist Postcard.

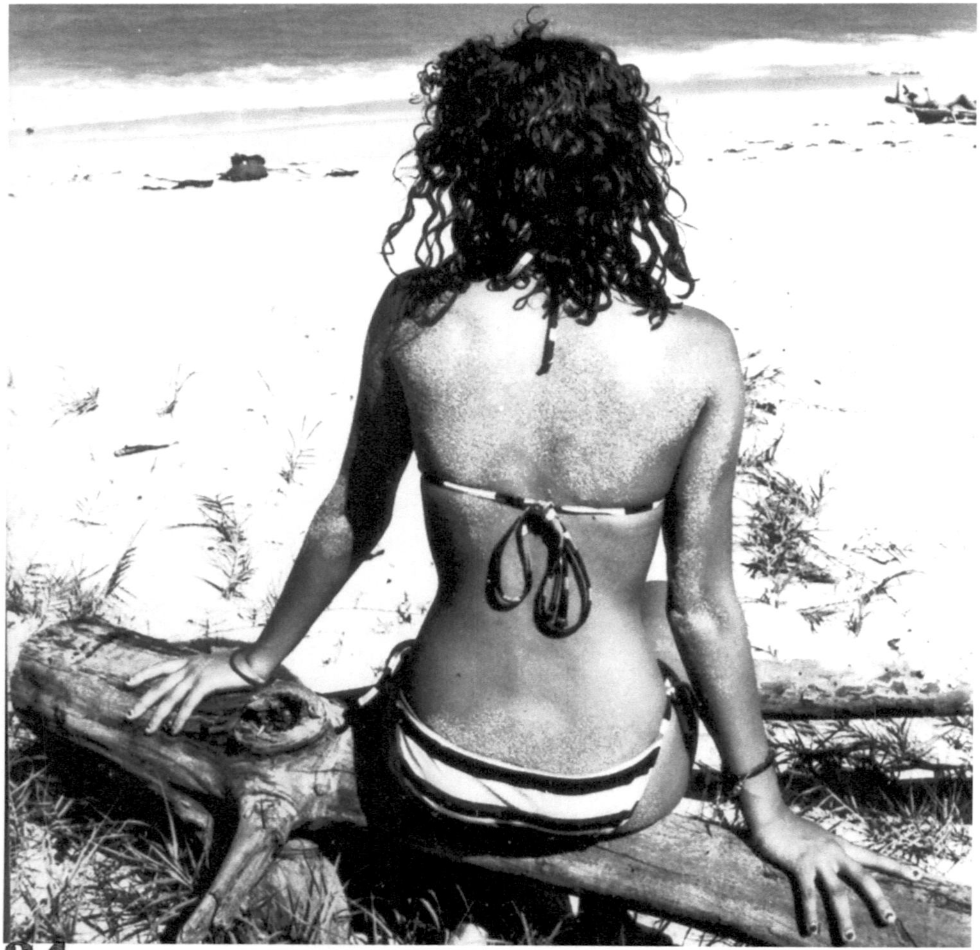

Postcard By Paige Testa, Student

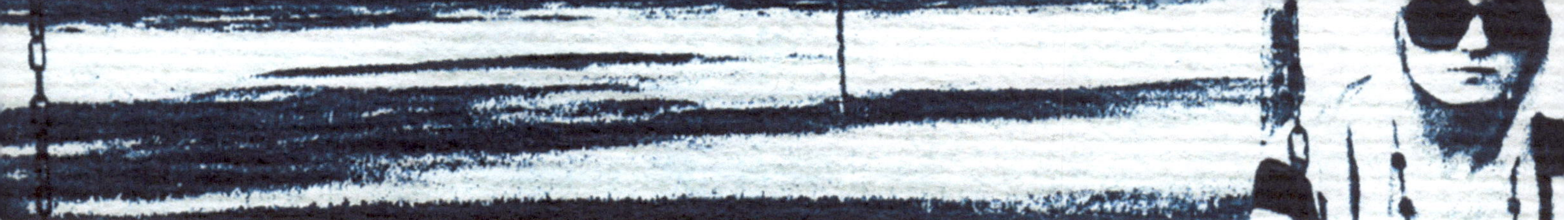

Postcard Six: Seeing Blue

The students will create an Artist Postcard using their knowledge of the alternative process cyanotype. The students will choose one of the following themes as the focus of their postcard: my favorite superhero or my favorite storybook character. The students will photograph the imagery for their cards using 35mm black and white film and a SLR camera. The students will create a five inch by seven inch print in the darkroom which they will then turn into an oversized negative using their knowledge of contact printing. The teacher will make photocopies of these large negatives onto transparency paper. The students will apply cyanotype chemicals onto a five inch by seven inch piece of watercolor paper. Finally, the students will expose their handmade light sensitive paper with their transparency negative on the surface underneath sunlight. Once the print has developed, the students will wash off the existing chemicals and allow the prints to dry before addressing them.

Postcard By Adrianna Jaramillo, Student

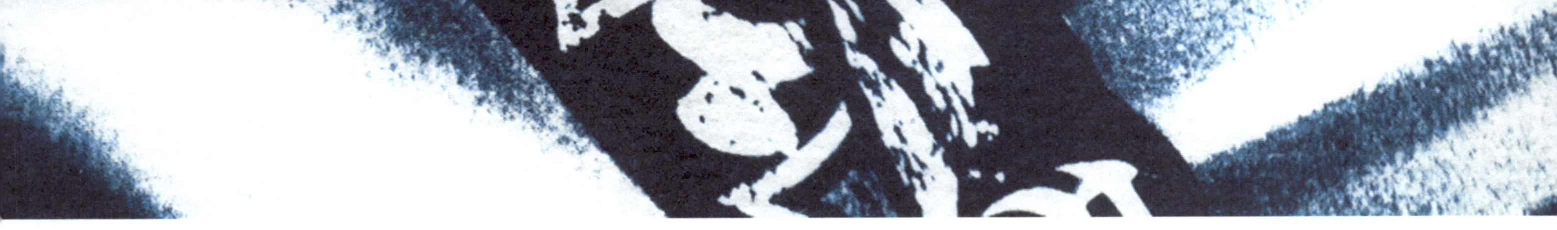

Teacher Procedure for Mixing Cyanotype Mixture:

Nettles (1992) provides a recipe for cyanotype that can be made in mass quantities a few days prior to the lesson intended. Part A and Part B must be stored separately in light tight bottles and then mixed together upon use. The cyanotype print works well on paper and organic fibers. It works best on watercolor paper.

Stock solution mixtures: You must wear gloves, goggles and an apron when mixing these chemicals. Use a weight and graduated cylinder to make sure that chemicals are completely accurate.

A. 50 grams Ferric Ammonium Citrate to 8 ounces distilled water
B. 35 grams Potassium Ferricyanide to 8 ounces distilled water

Procedure for application to paper:

Preparation: In a dimly lit room, mix equal volumes of part A and part B together. Use this the same day.

Sensitize the Surface: Cover your work area with clean paper. Under low light, apply a thin, even coat onto paper with a clean foam brush. Do not reuse the brush for any other process.

Dry Coated Material: Still under dim light, dry the surface of the paper with a hair drier or fan. If you would like to air dry the paper, this must be done in complete darkness.

Storage: When you have dried the paper completely, stack into a light-tight box for later use.

Prior to having the students do cyanotype printing in class, it is recommended to test your chemical mixture. Take several pieces of prepared watercolor and expose them to light. Time how long it takes before the paper has the appearance of a dark blue hue, similar to that of a blueprint. After your paper has been exposed sufficiently, wash it thoroughly in cool running water making sure to remove all excess chemical. The chemical itself has a yellowish hue that must be completely removed. Allow to dry. **(p. 34)**

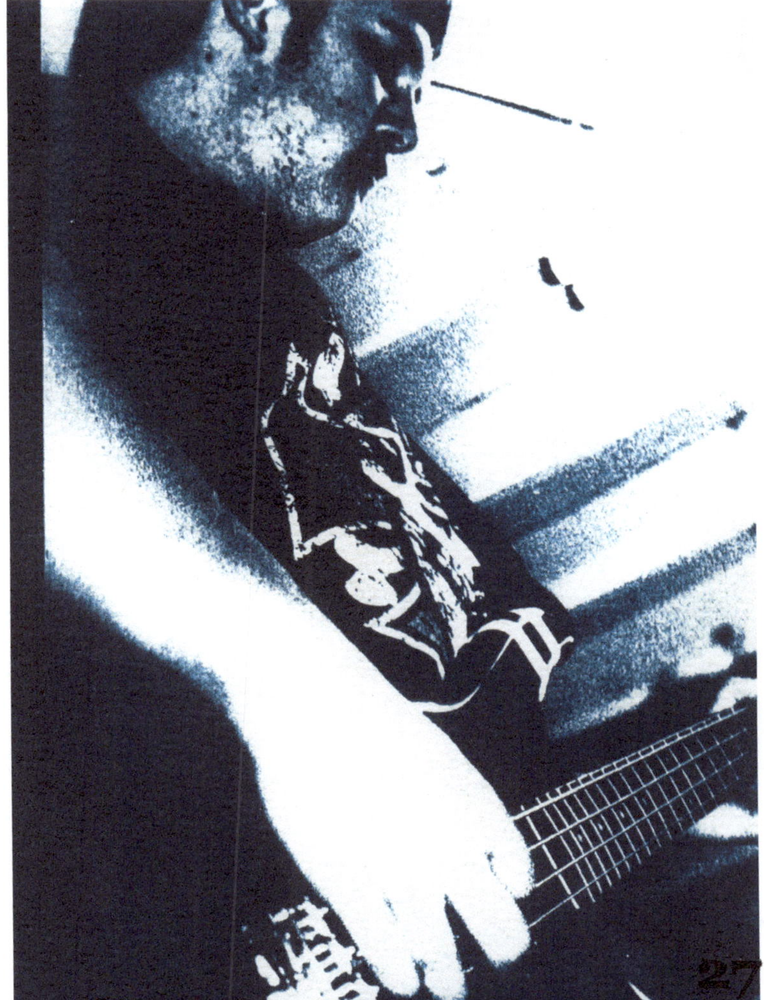

Postcard By Jacob Brantley, Student

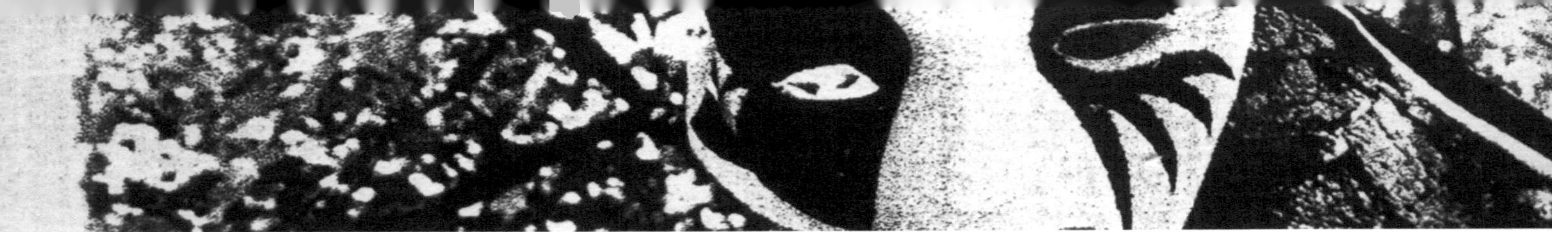

Postcard Seven: Seeing Brown

The students will create an Artist Postcard using their knowledge of the alternative process Van Dyke Brown. The students will look at a variety of vintage images from local antique shops. The students will compare and contrast the images to their own snapshots. The students will create a vintage image of their own depicting current times for future generations. The students will shoot their vintage shot using 35mm black and white film and a SLR camera. The students will create a five inch by seven inch print in the darkroom which they will then turn into an oversized negative using their knowledge of contact printing. The teacher will make photocopies of these large negatives onto transparency paper. The students will apply Van Dyke Brown chemicals onto a five inch by seven inch piece of watercolor paper. Finally, the students will expose their handmade light sensitive paper with their transparency negative on the surface underneath sunlight. Once the print has developed, the students will wash off the existing chemicals and allow the prints to dry before addressing them.

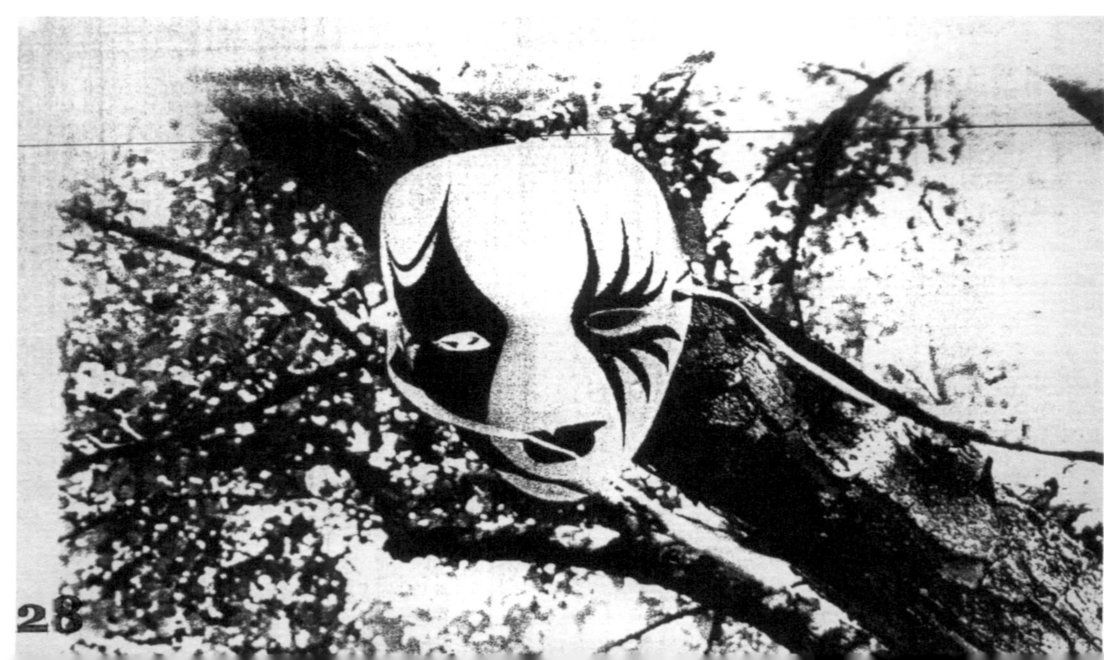

Postcard By
Paige Testa, Student

Teacher Procedure for Mixing Vandyke Brown Mixture:

Nettles (1992) provides a recipe for Van Dyke Brown that can be made in mass quantities a few days prior to the lesson intended. The solution must be stored in light tight bottles. The Van Dyke Brown print works well on paper and organic fibers. It works best on watercolor paper.

Stock solution mixture: You must wear gloves, goggles and an apron when mixing these chemicals. Use a weight and graduated cylinder to make sure that chemicals are completely accurate.

A. 90 grams Ferric Ammonium Citrate to 8 ounces distilled water
B. 15 grams of Tartaric Acid to 8 ounces distilled water
C. 37.5 grams of Silver Nitrate to 8 ounces distilled water

Procedure for application to paper:

Preparation: In a dimly lit room, combine the Ferric Ammonium Citrate and the Tartaric Acid solution. Slowly and carefully add the Silver Nitrate. Add enough distilled water to the mixture to make 32 ounces of solution.

Sensitize the Surface: Cover your work area with clean paper. Under low light, apply a thin, even coat onto paper with a clean foam brush. Don't reuse the brush for any other process.

Dry Coated Material: Still under dim light, dry the surface of the paper with a hair drier or fan. If you would like to air dry the paper, this must be done in complete darkness.

Storage: When you have dried the paper completely, stack into a light-tight box for later use.

Prior to having the students do Van Dyke printing in class, it is recommended to test your chemical mixture. Take several pieces of prepared watercolor and expose them to light. Time how long it takes before the paper has the appearance of a dark brown hue. After your paper has been exposed sufficiently, wash it thoroughly in cool running water making sure to remove all excess chemical. Allow to dry. (p. 35)

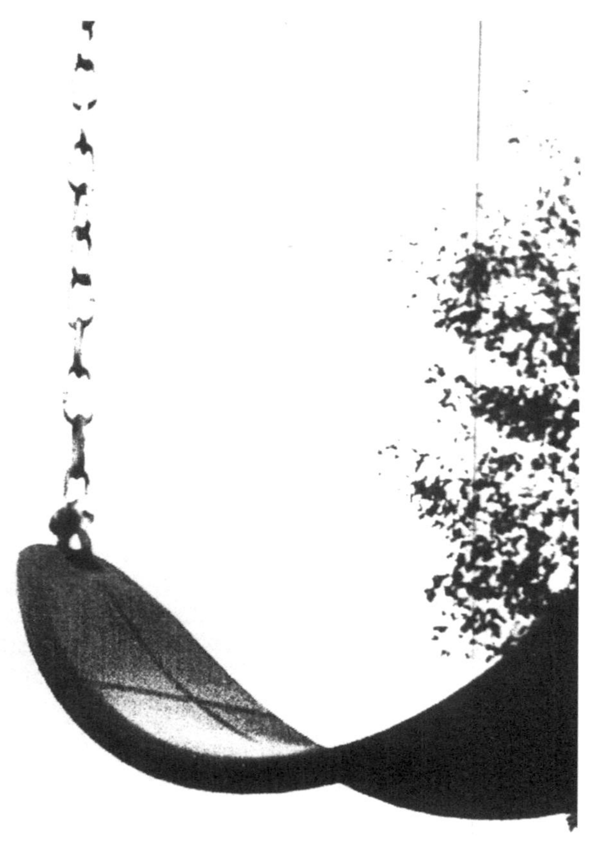

Postcard By Adrianna Jaramillo

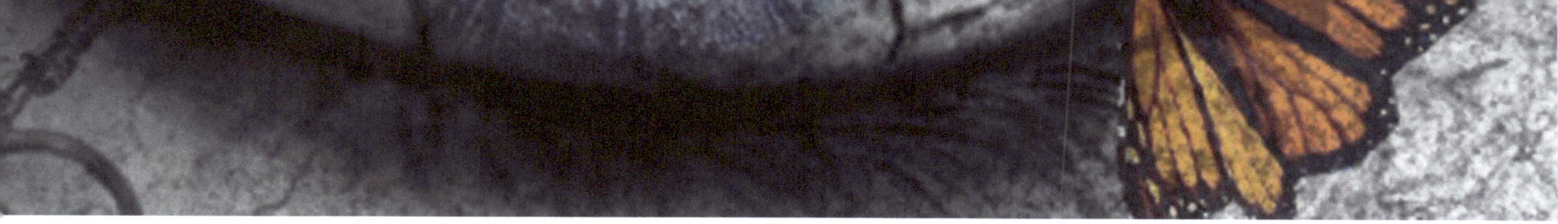

Postcard Eight: Photographic Montage

The students will create an Artist Postcard that demonstrates their understanding and skills in creating a photographic montage. The students will combine at least three of their own photographs with found objects to create a composition that focuses around one of the following themes: my world in an image, the most terrifying nightmare, how the rest of the world sees me. The students will adhere their montage onto cardstock.

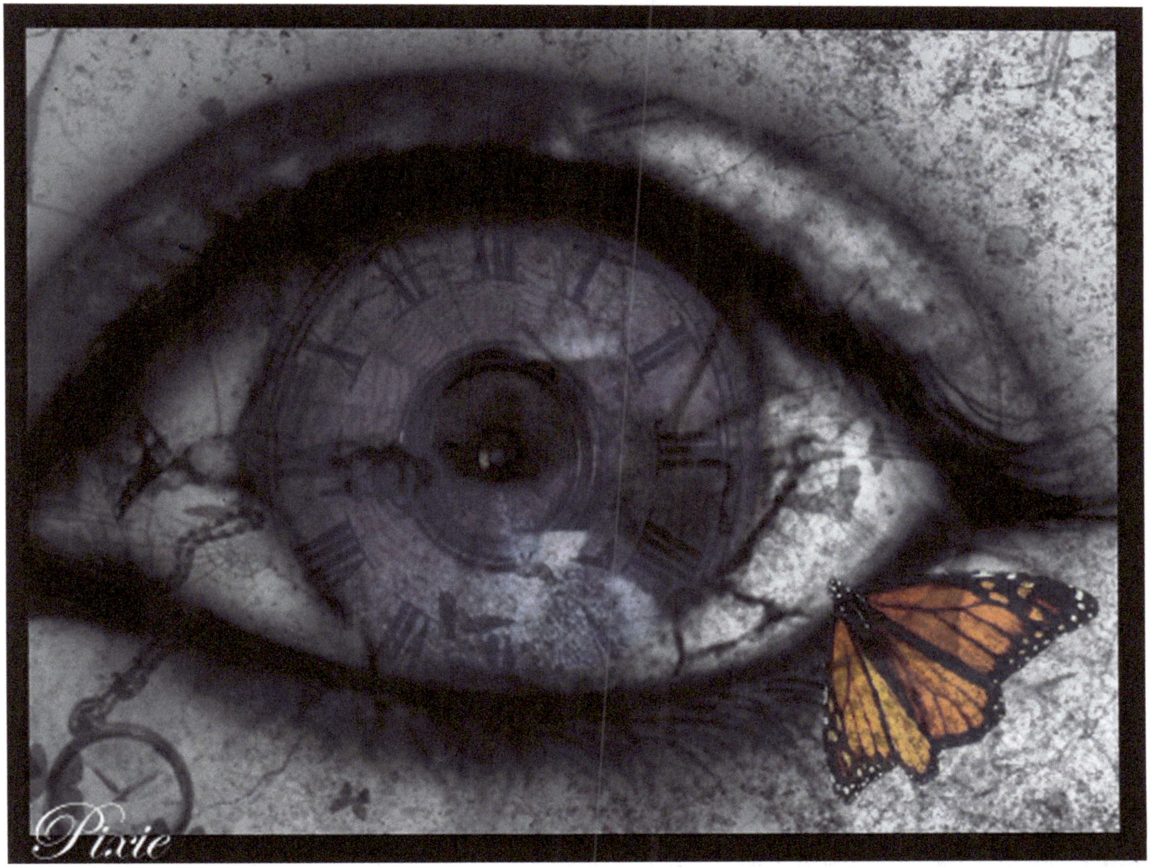

Postcard By Nancy Nunez, Student

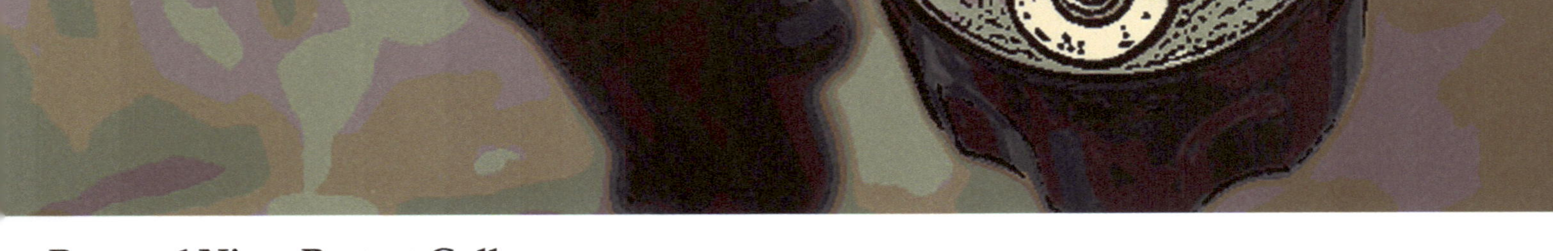

Postcard Nine: Protest Collage

The students will create an Artist Postcard that demonstrates their feelings on a controversial issue using collage as their medium. The students will choose a controversial issue that they feel passionately about and create a composition that integrates at least three of their own digital or film images with found objects. The students will adhere their montage onto cardstock.

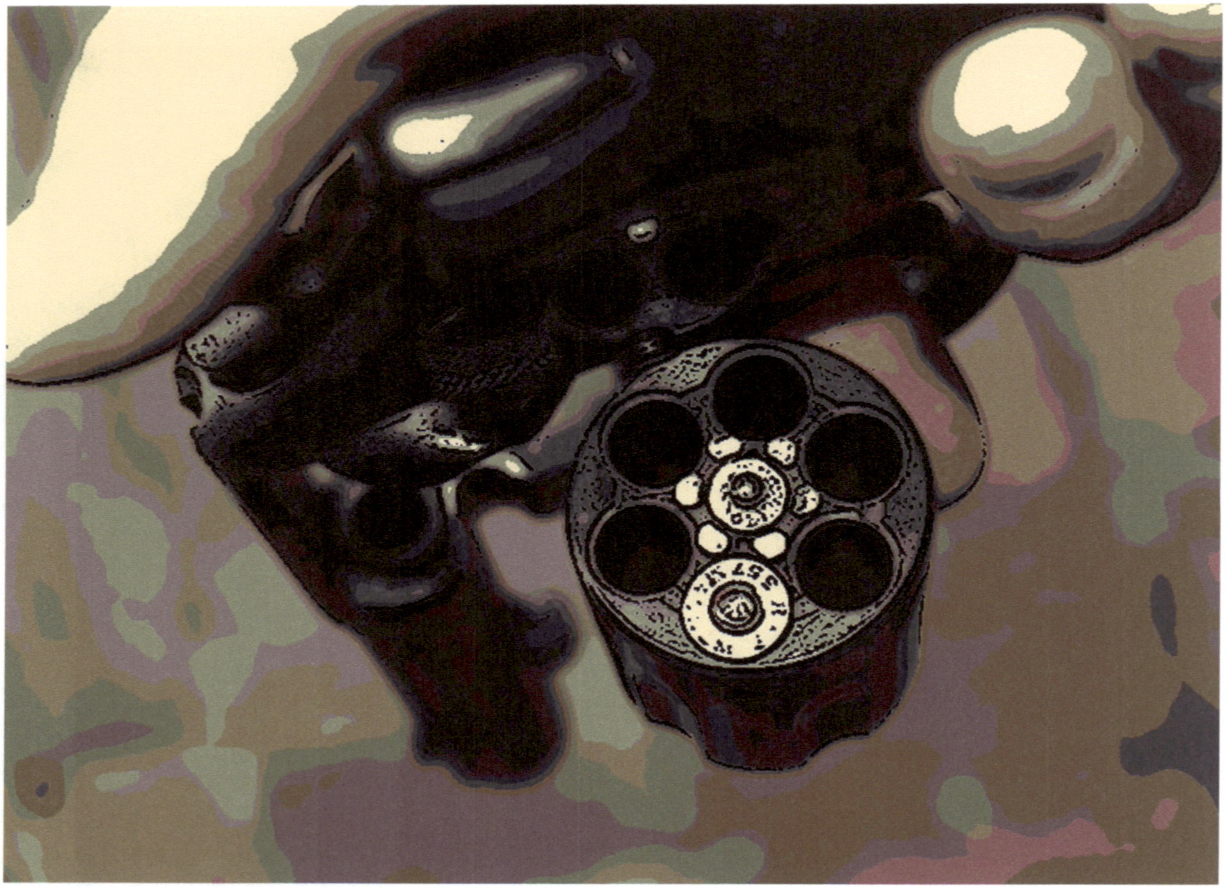

Postcard By Jacob Brantley, Student

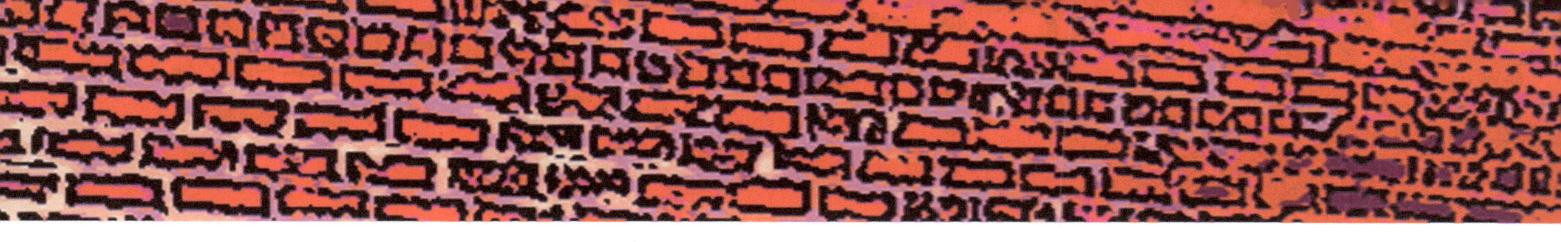

Postcard Ten: Freestyle

The students will create an Artist Postcard of their own design and inspiration. The students are welcome to explore any and all media and processes they have learned during the course of their artistic experience to create a composition that is visually engaging and interesting.

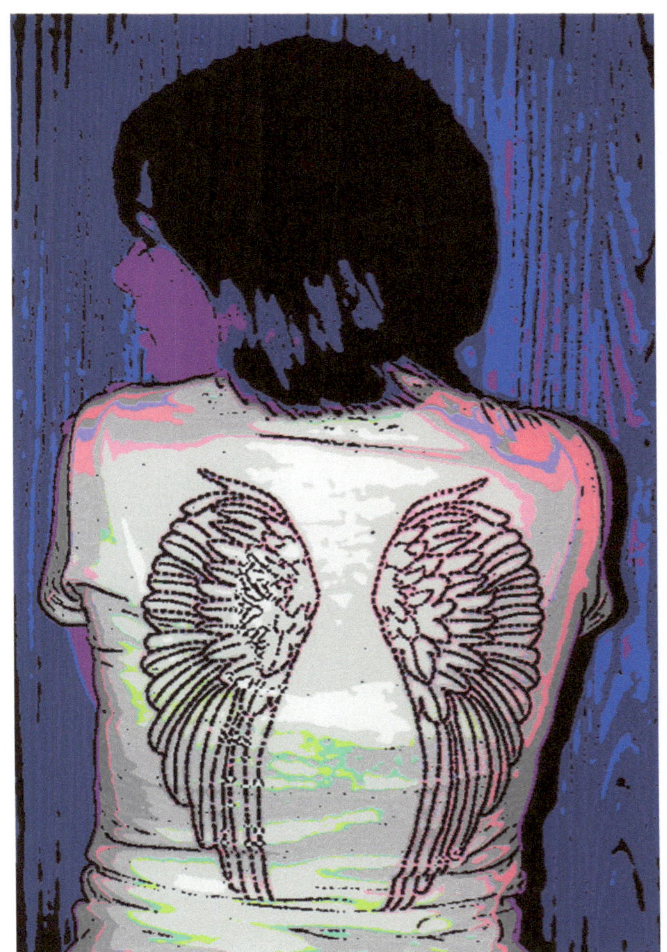

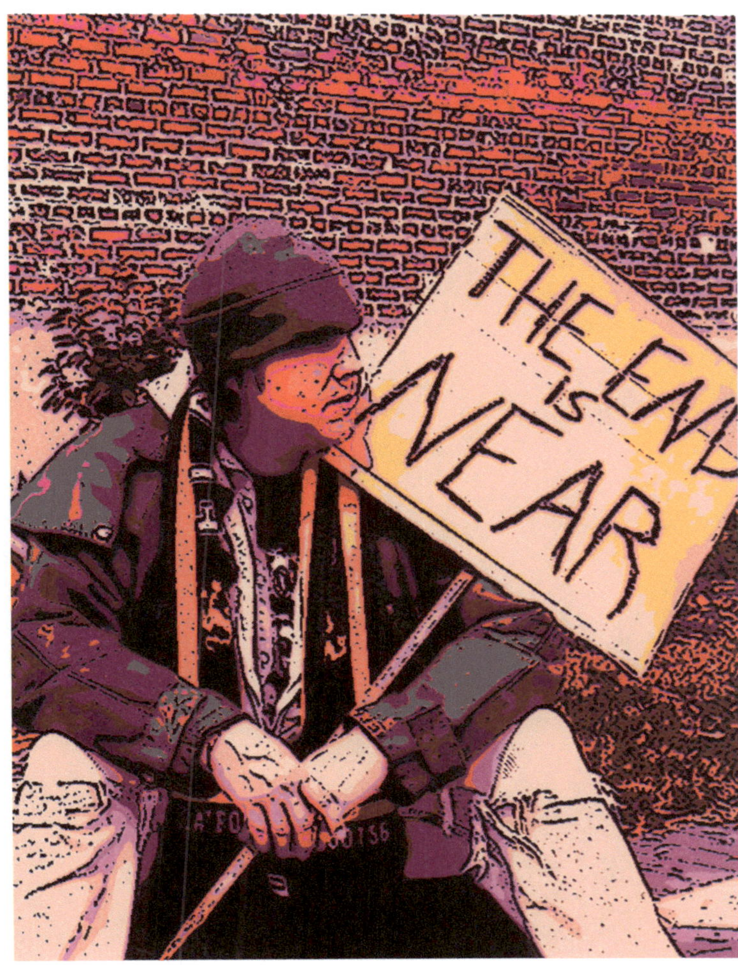

Postcards By Jacob Brantley, Student

Postcard Gallery...

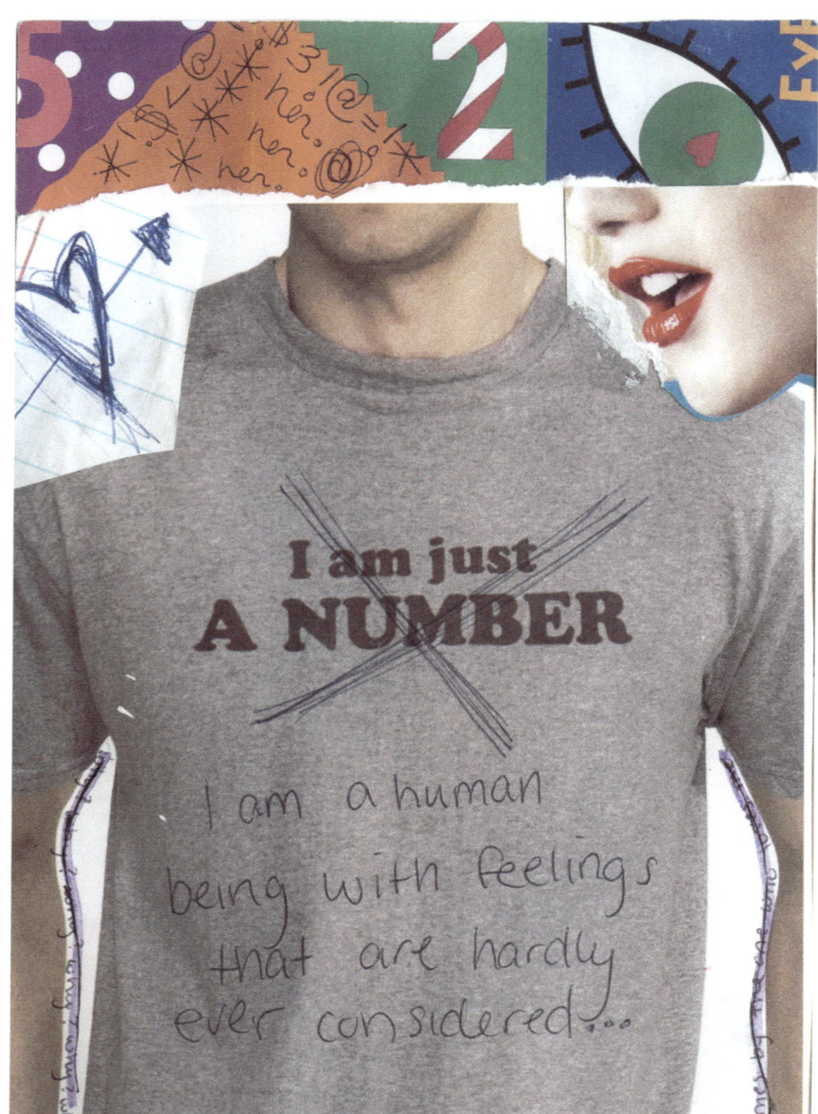

Postcard By
Paige Testa, Student

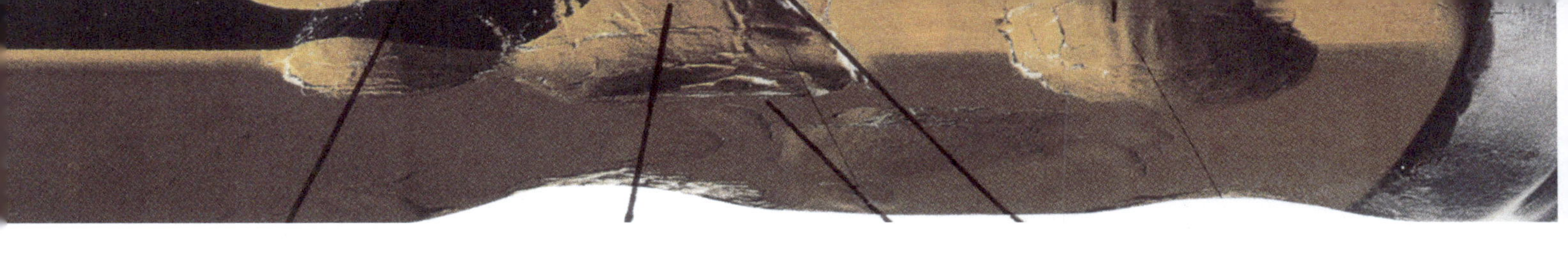

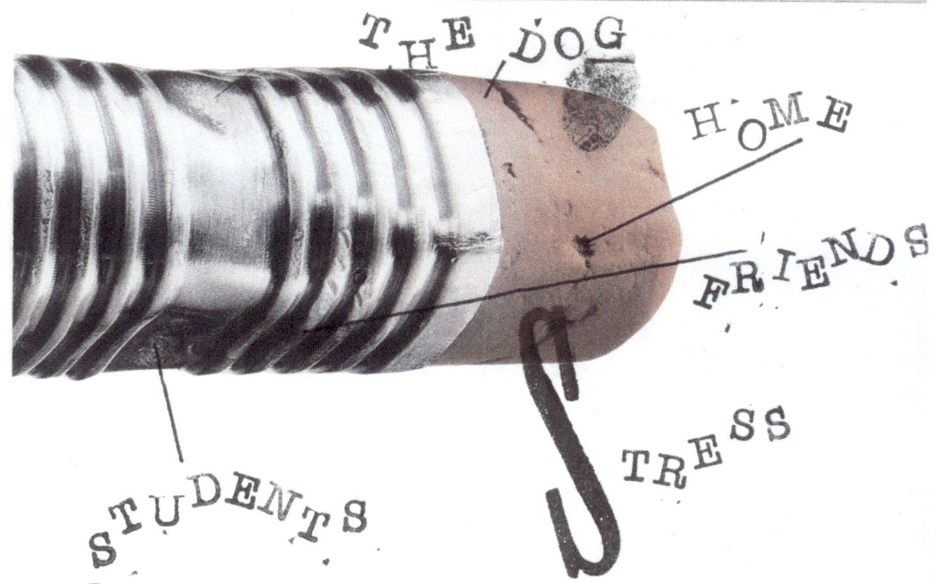

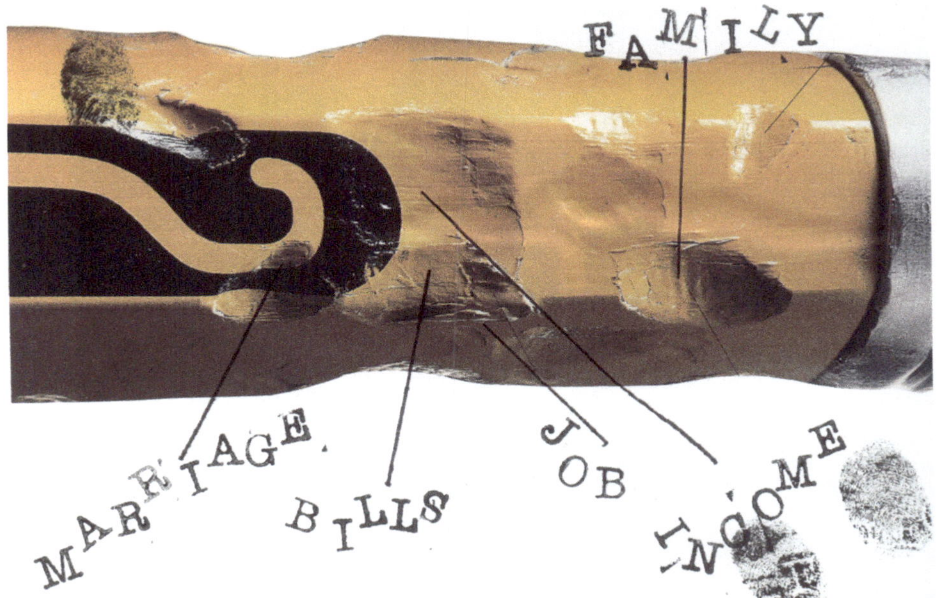

Postcards By
Sarah Cress

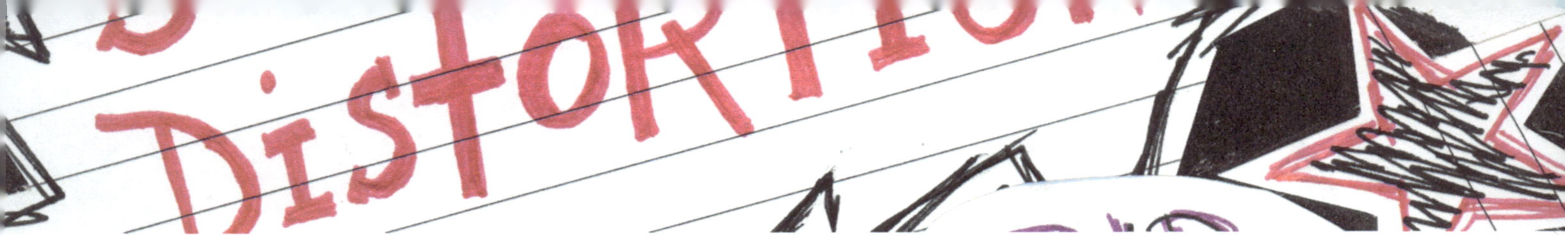

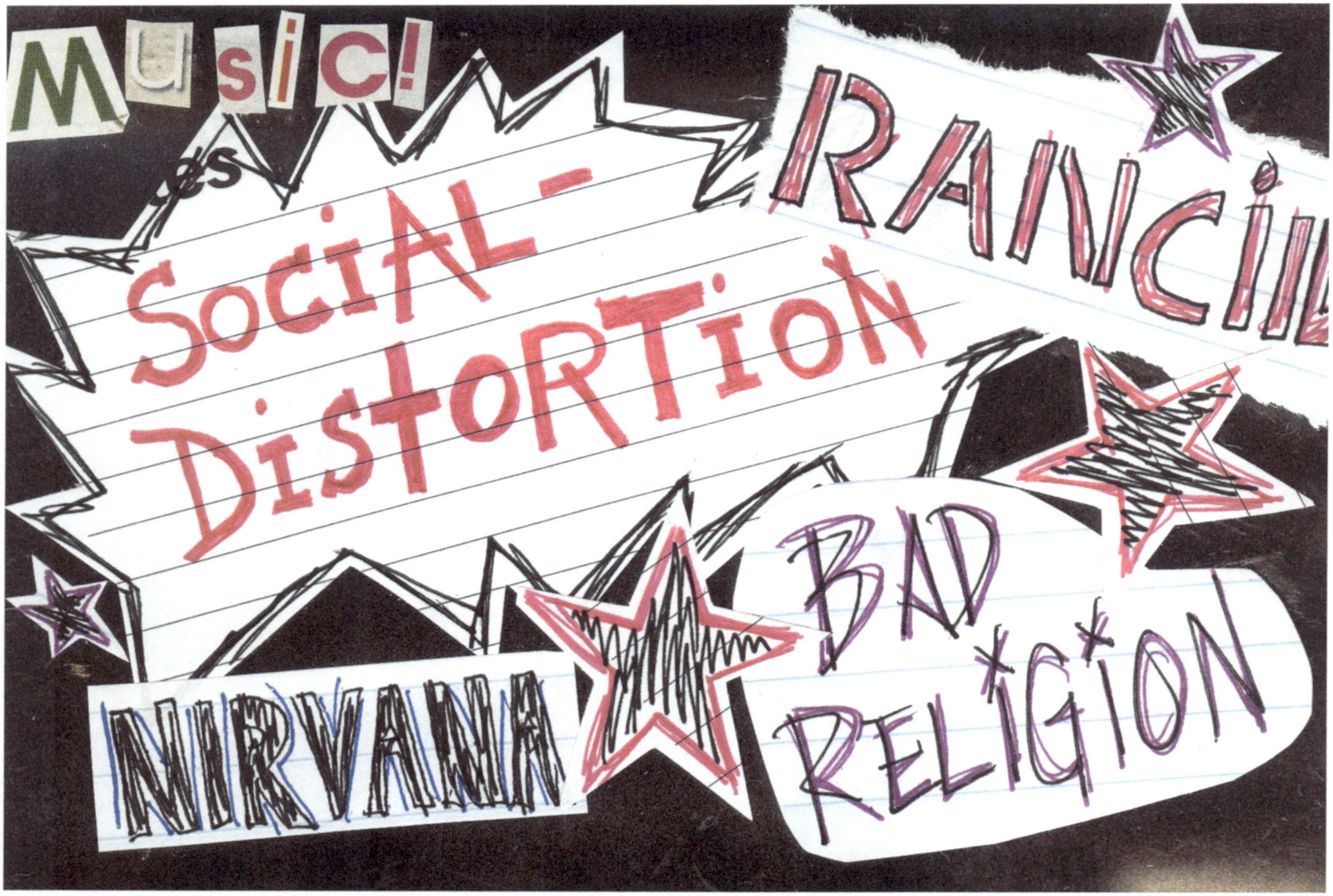

Postcard By Rebecca Humann, Student

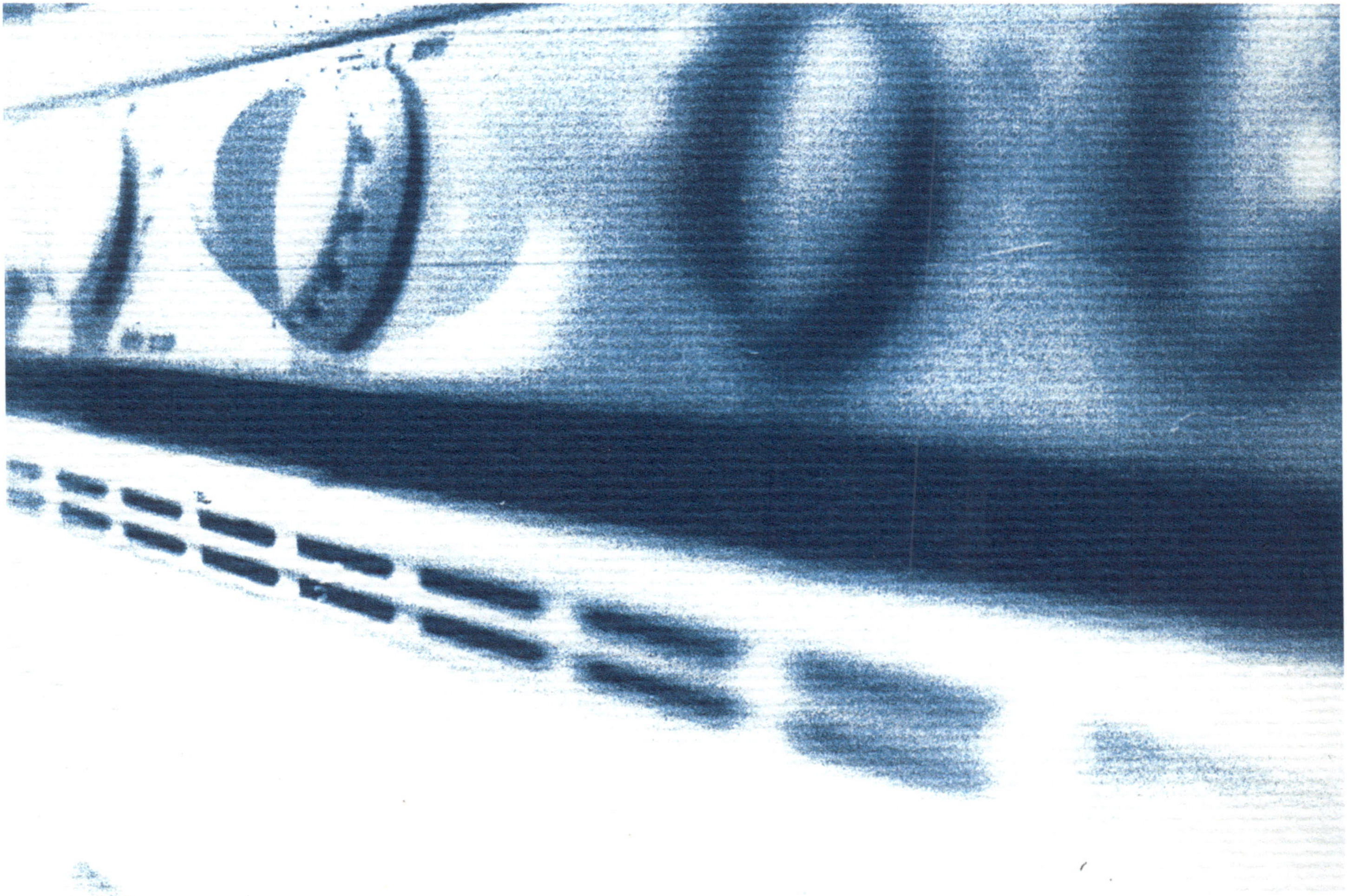

Postcard By Tricia Bohannan, Student

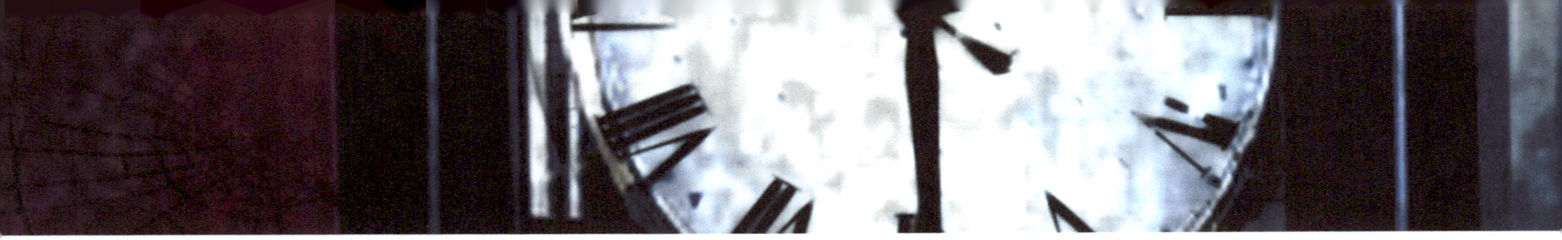

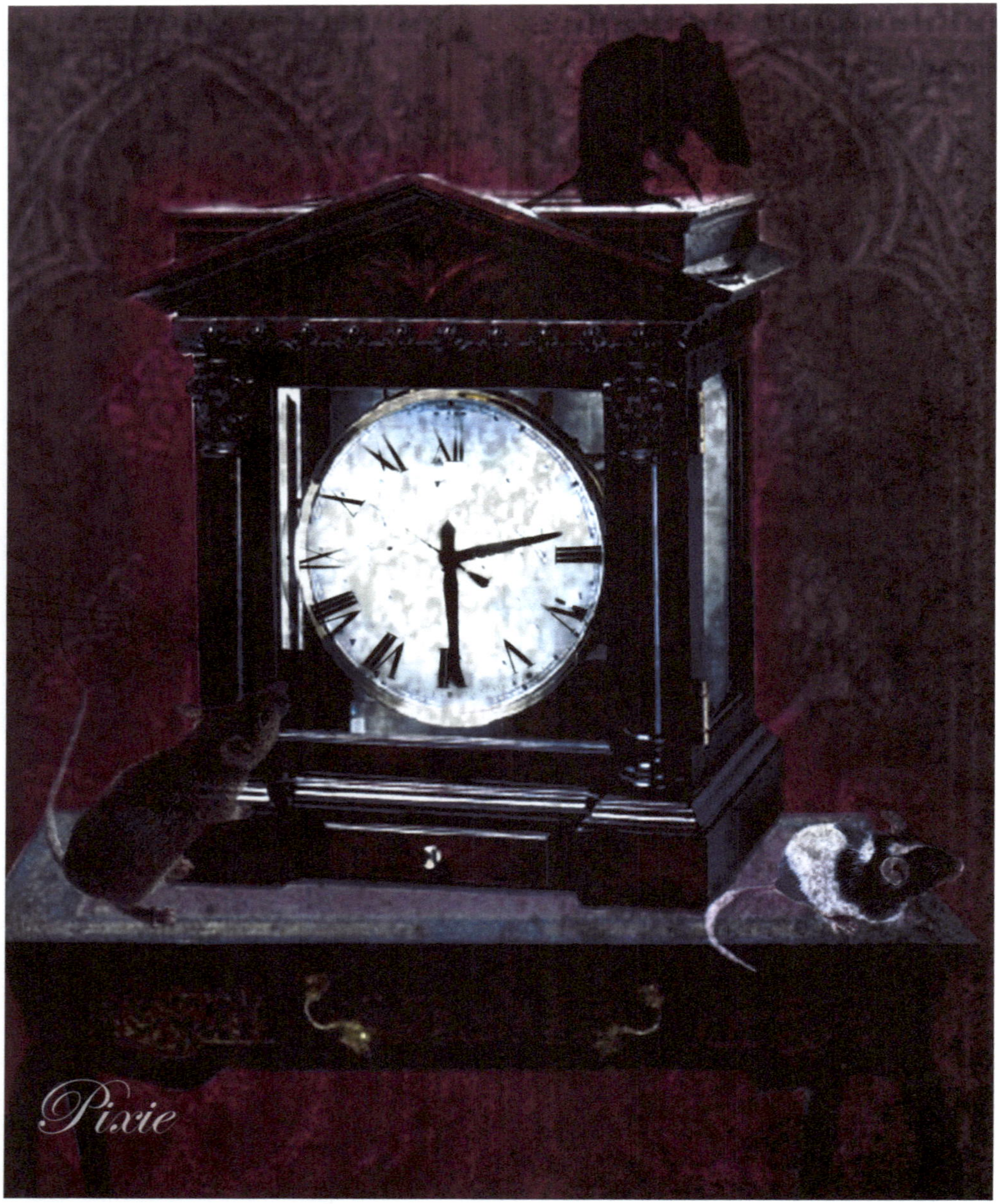

Pixie

Postcard By Nancy Nunez, Student

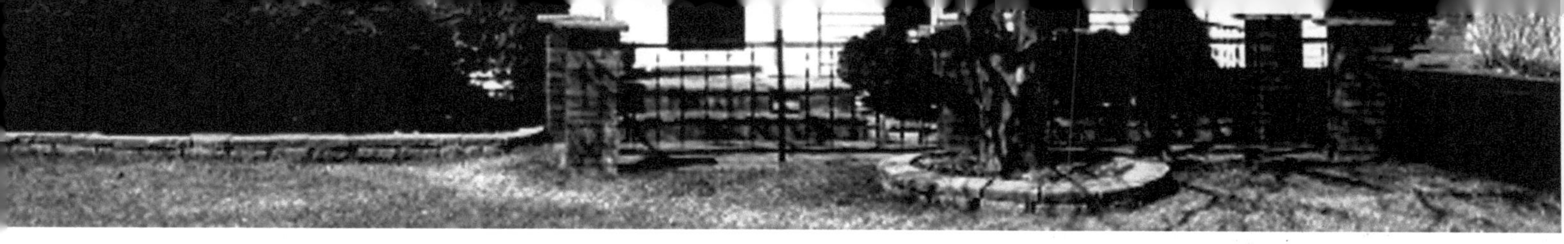

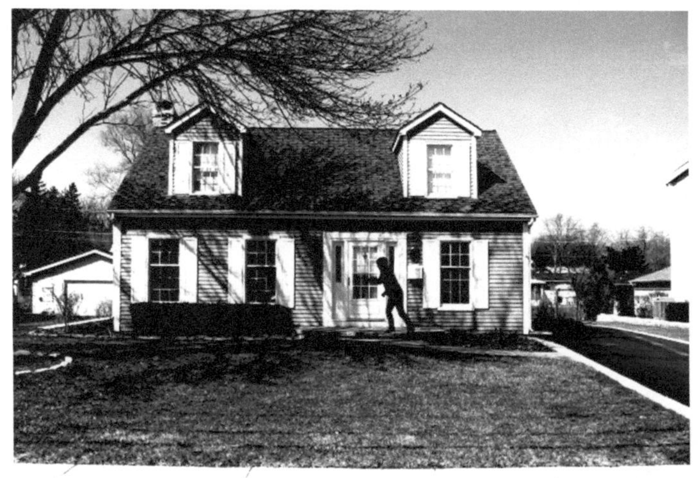

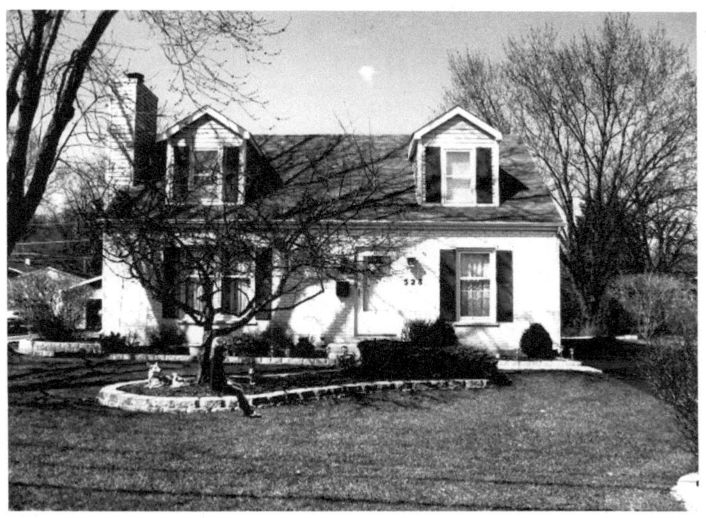

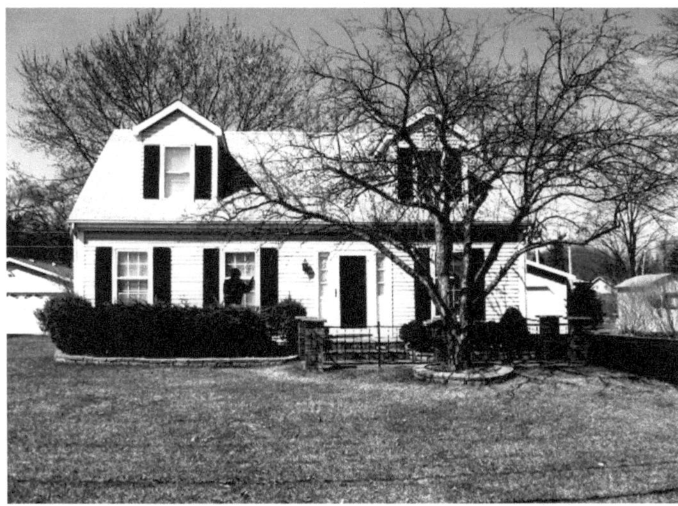

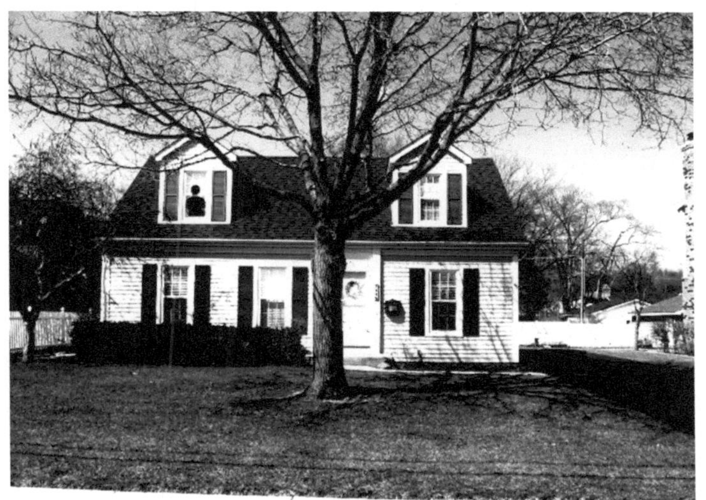

Postcards By Joey Ouimet, Student

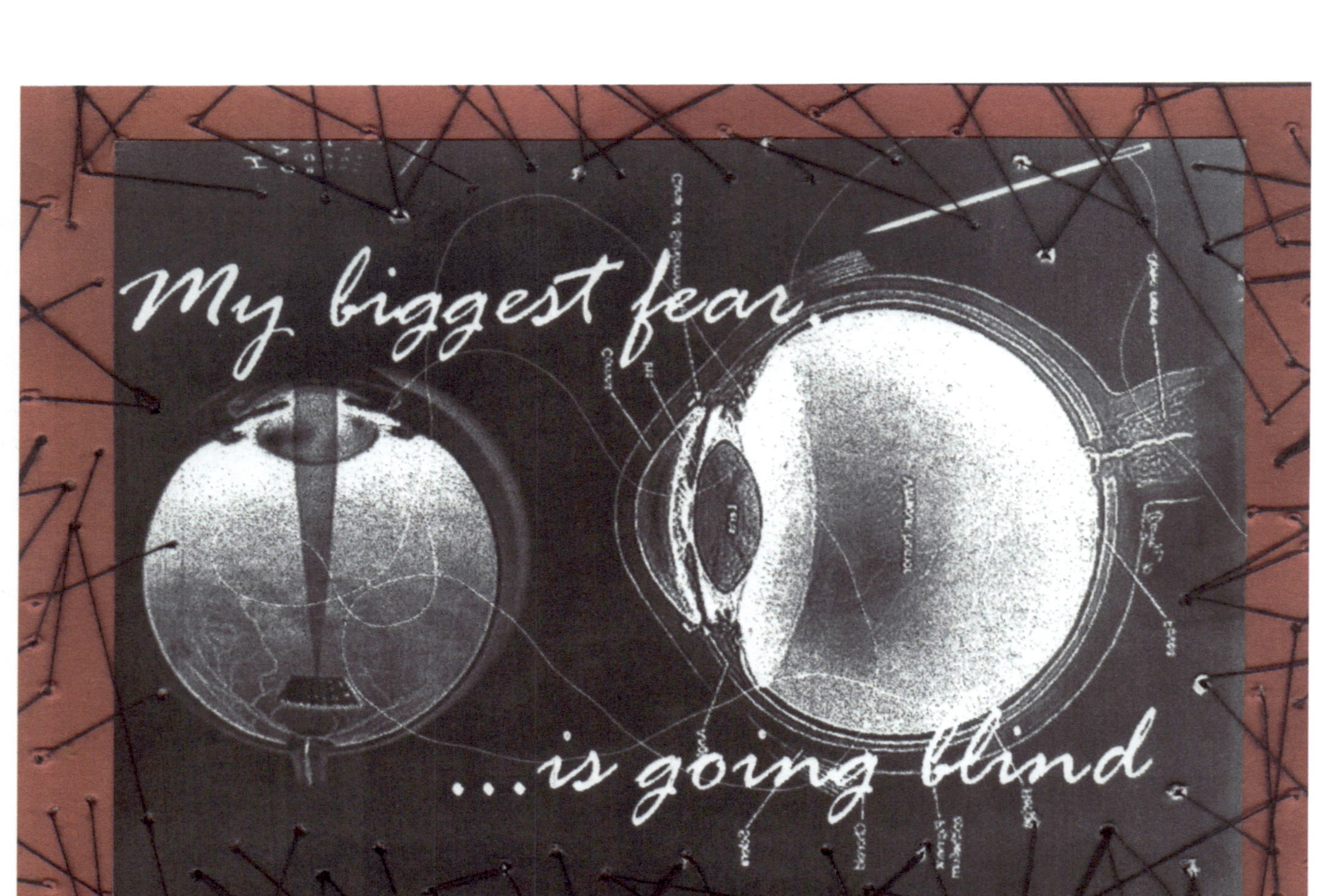

Postcard By Sarah Cress

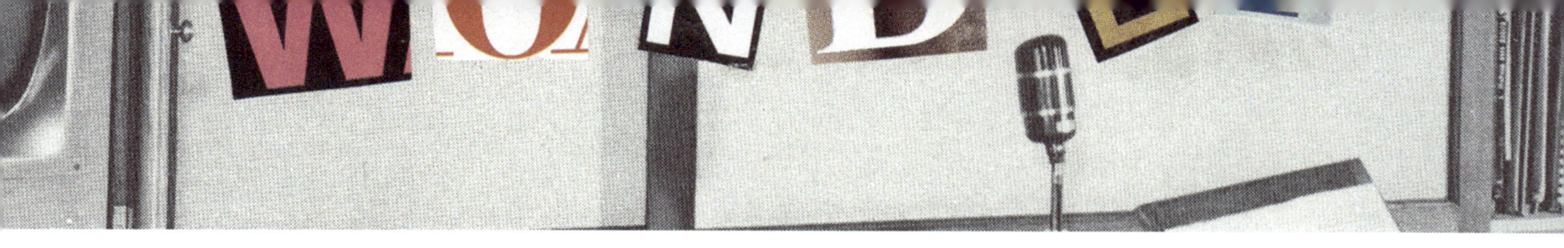

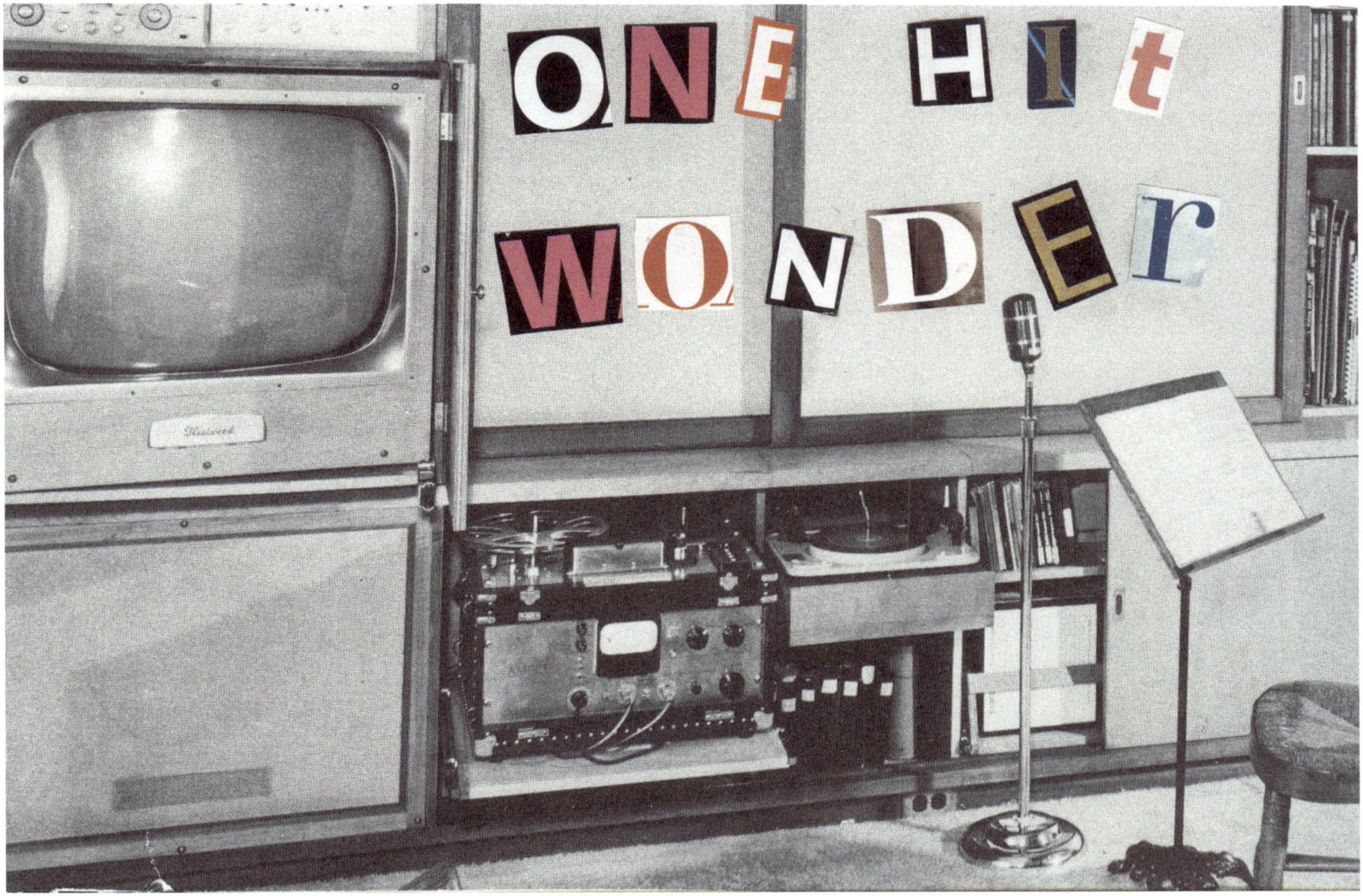

ONE HIt WONDEr

Postcard By Lindsey Herdrich, Student

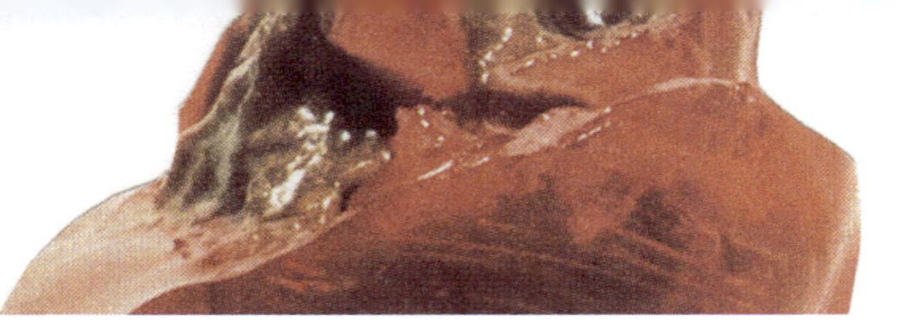

girl I lived i

When I was a little girl I lived in the moment at all times. Never did I think about my career or marriage or where I might be in 10 years. Today I can't keep those things off my mind . . . I wish I could live in the moment again.

Postcards By Sarah Cress

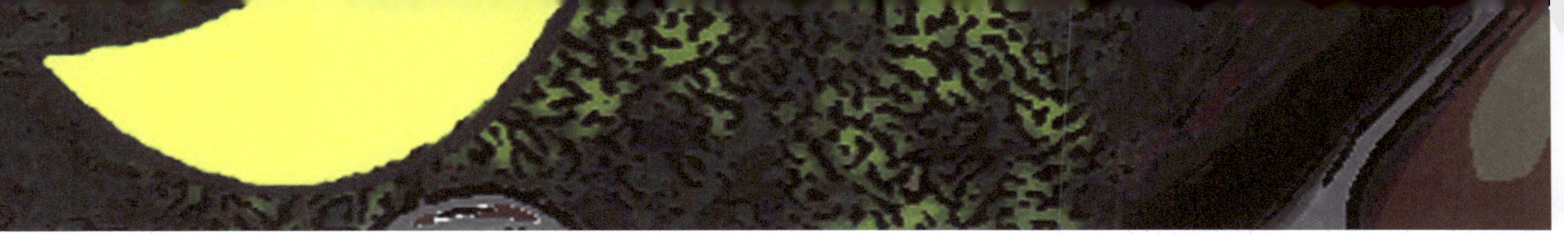

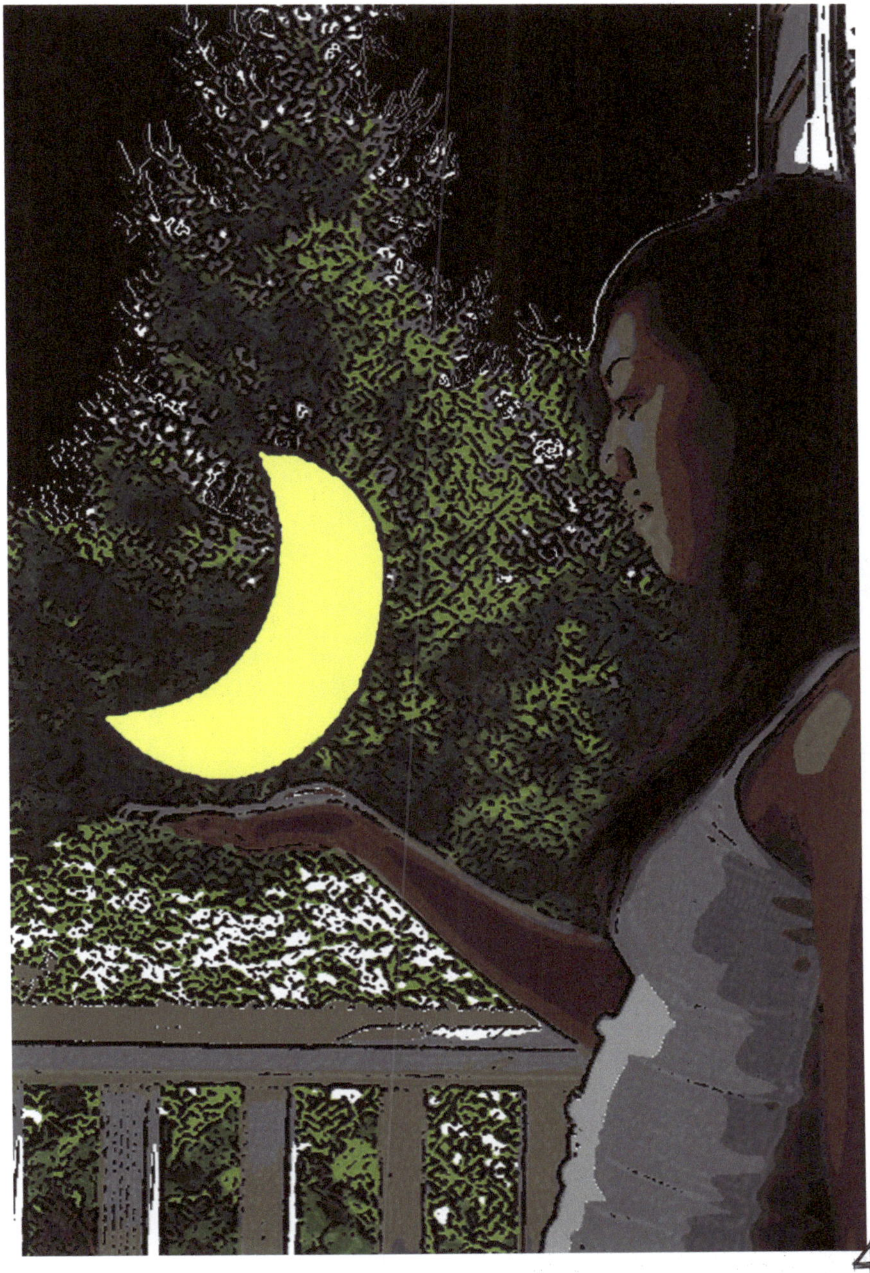

*Postcard By
Jacob Brantley,
Student*

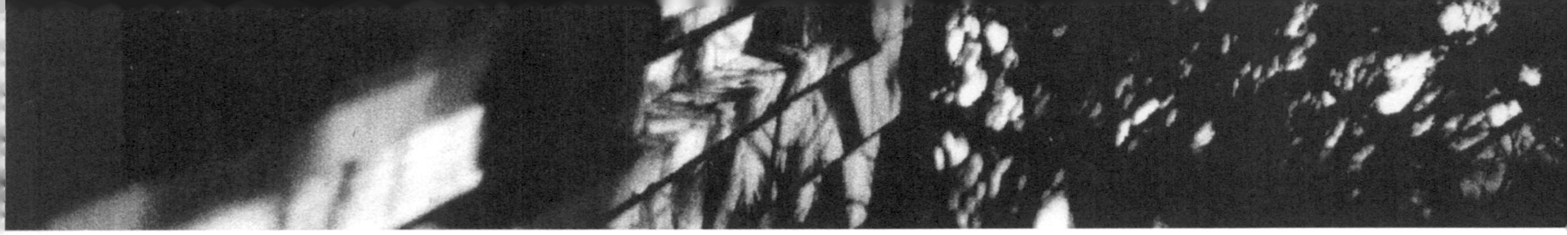

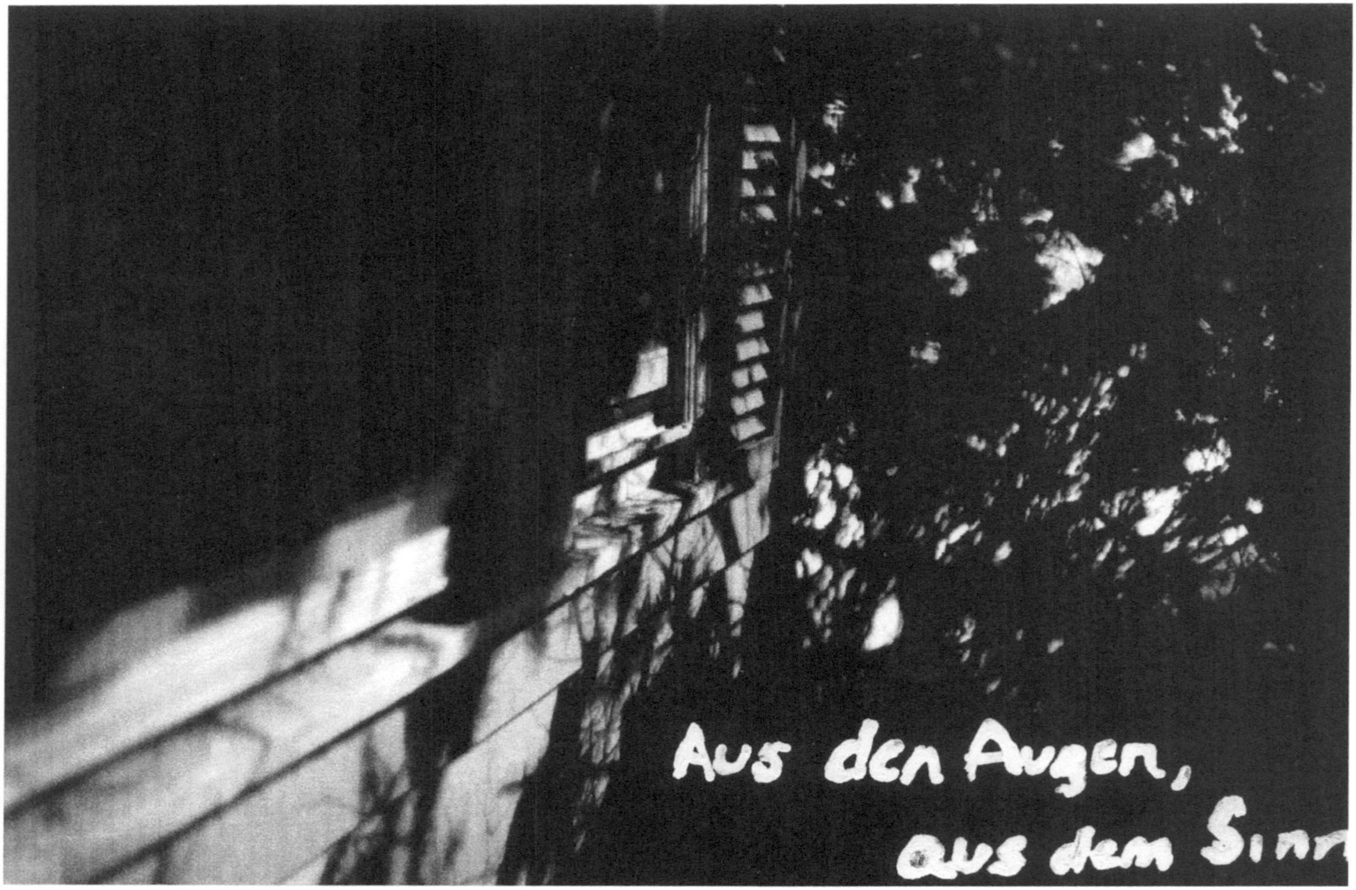

Postcard By Sarah Chambers, Student

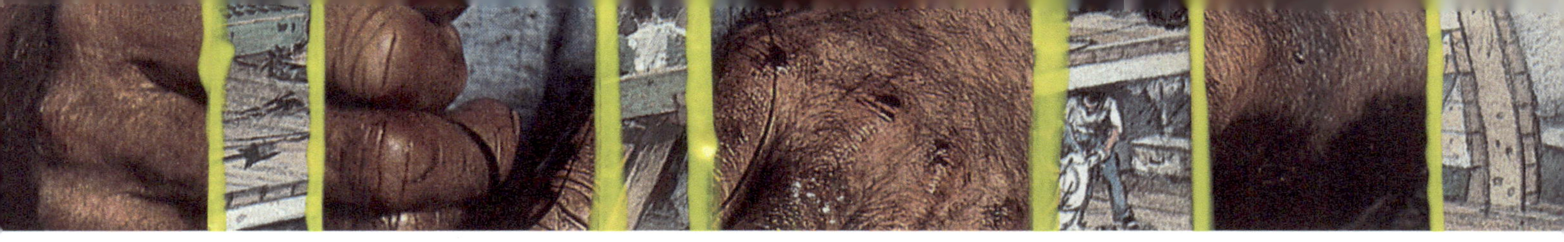

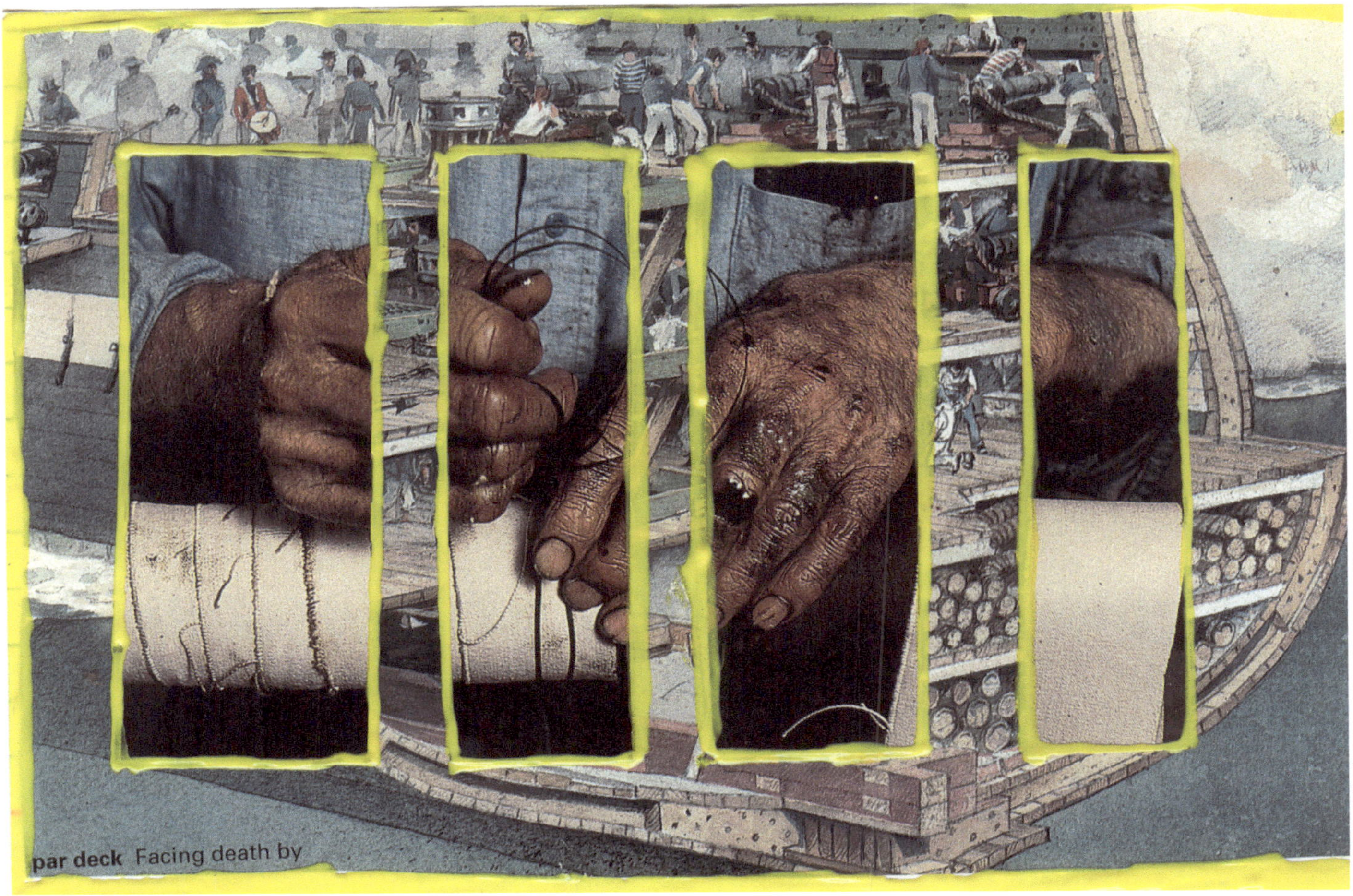

par deck Facing death by

Postcard By Paige Testa, Student

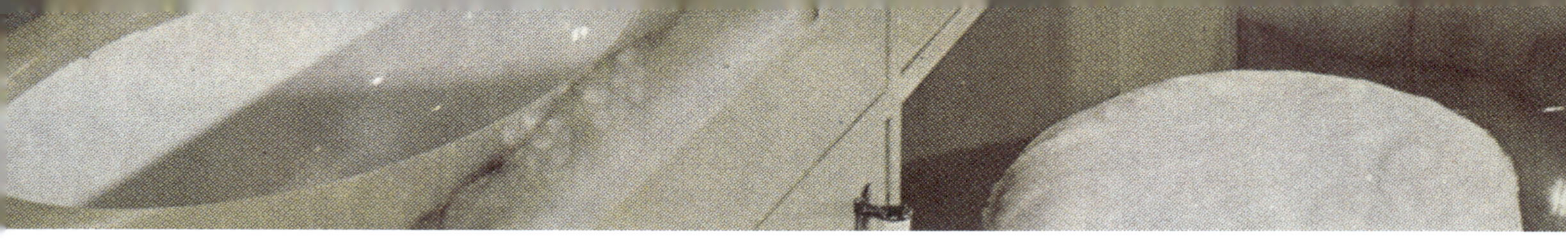

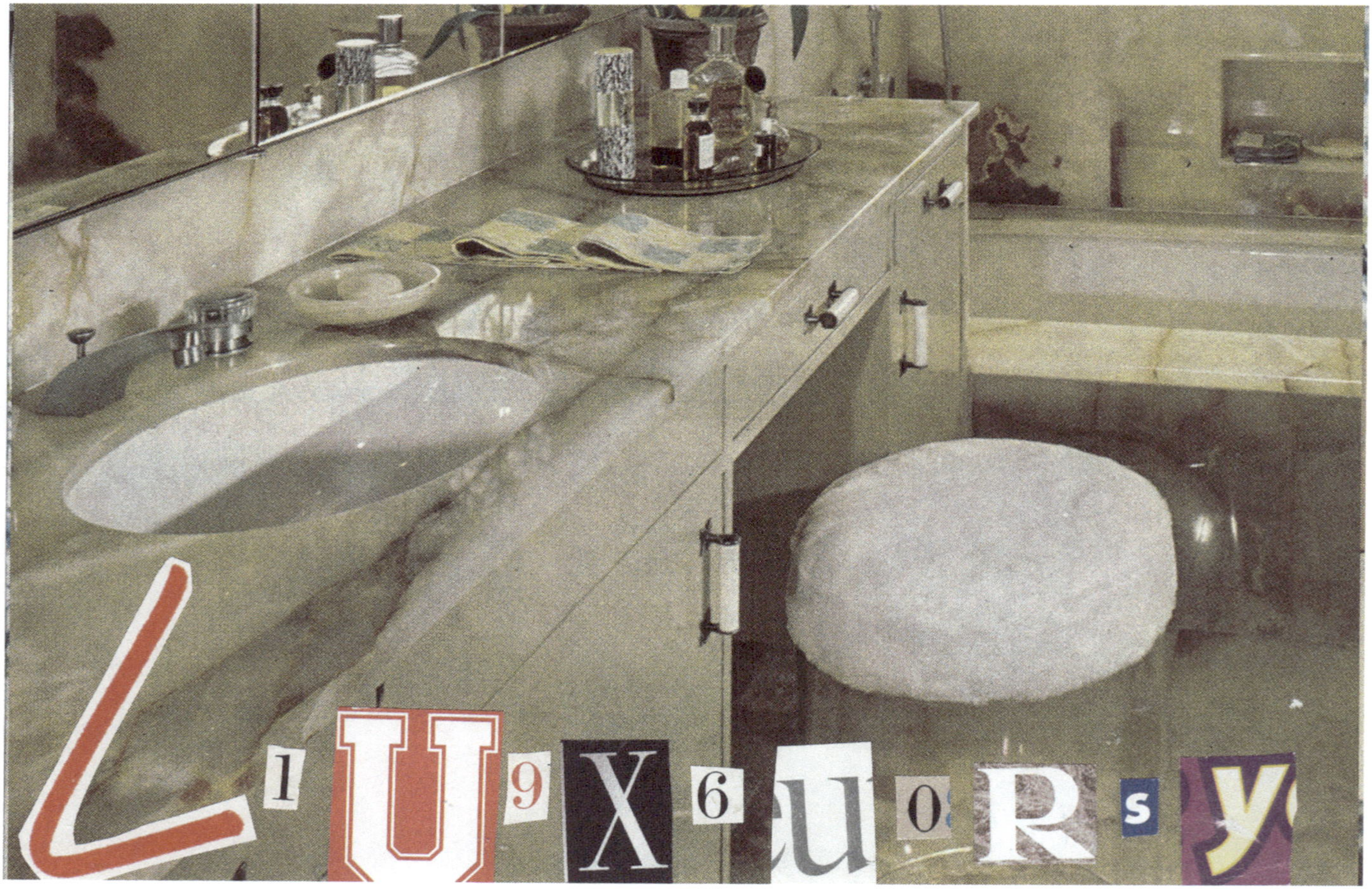

Postcard By Lindsey Herdrich, Student

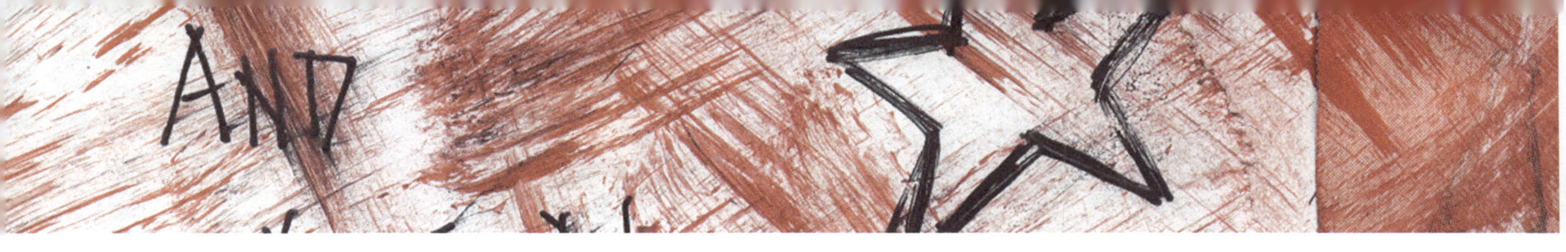

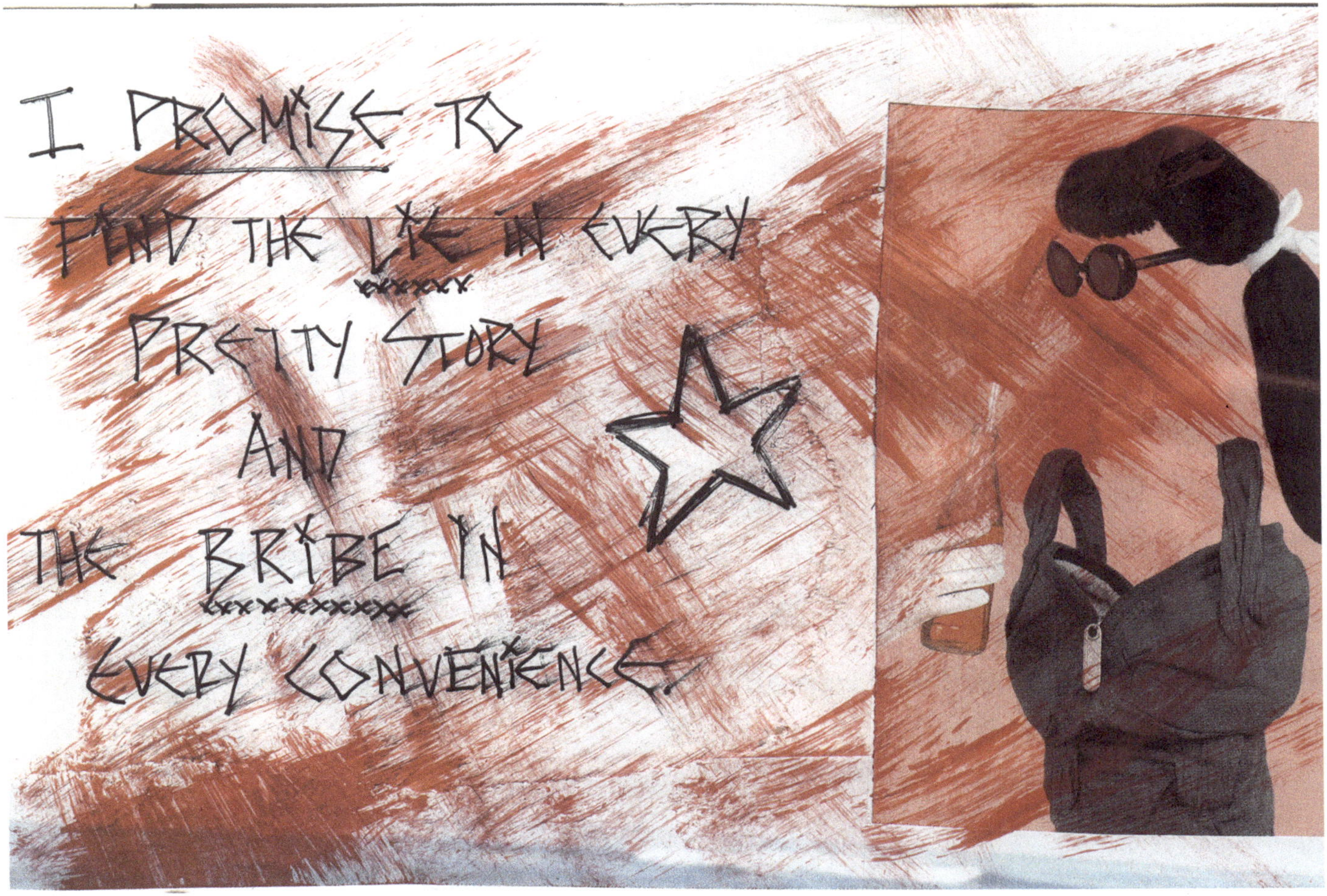

I PROMISE TO
FIND THE LIE IN EVERY
PRETTY STORY
AND
THE BRIBE IN
EVERY CONVENIENCE.

Postcard By Rebecca Humann, Student

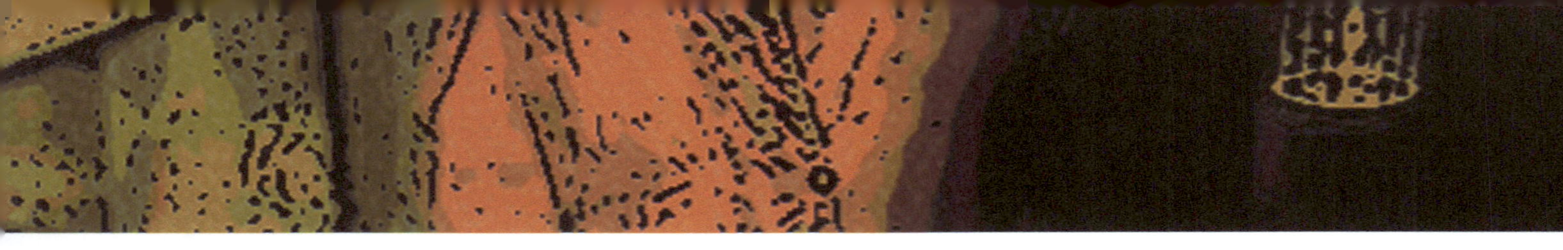

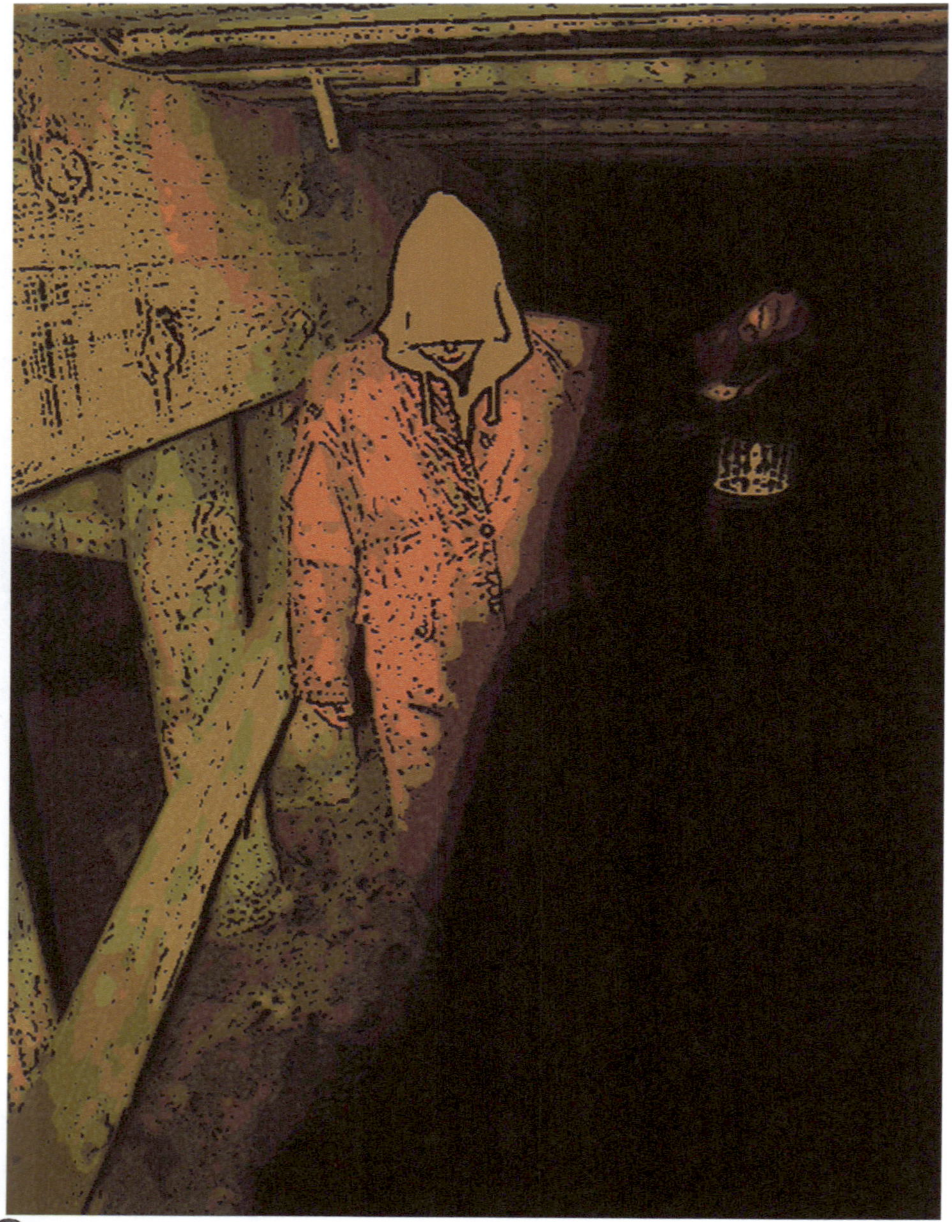

Postcard By Jacob Brantley, Student

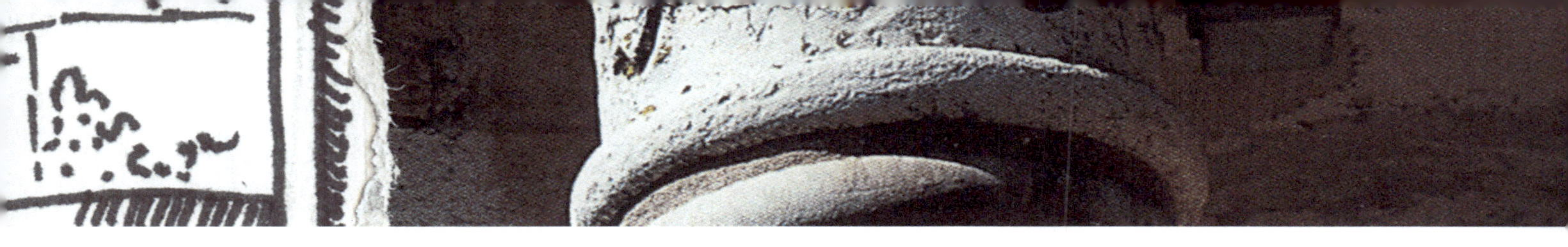

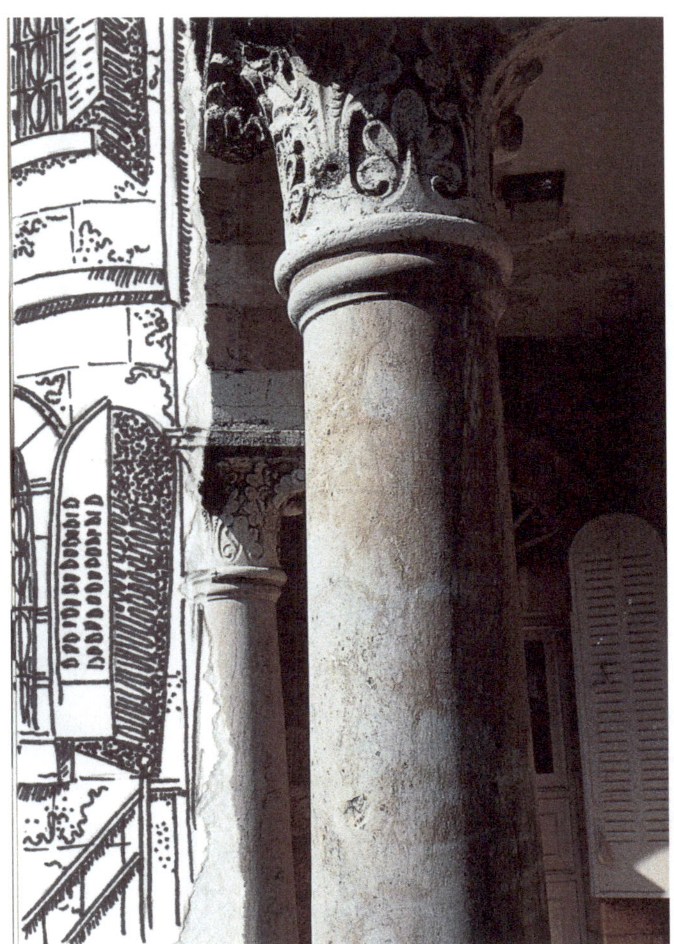

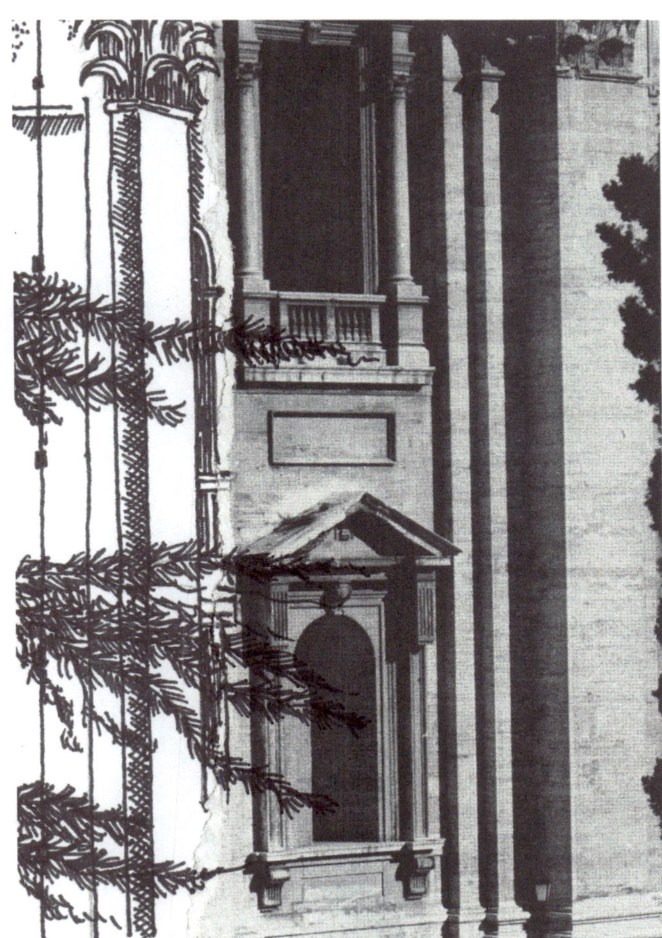

Postcards By Sarah Cress

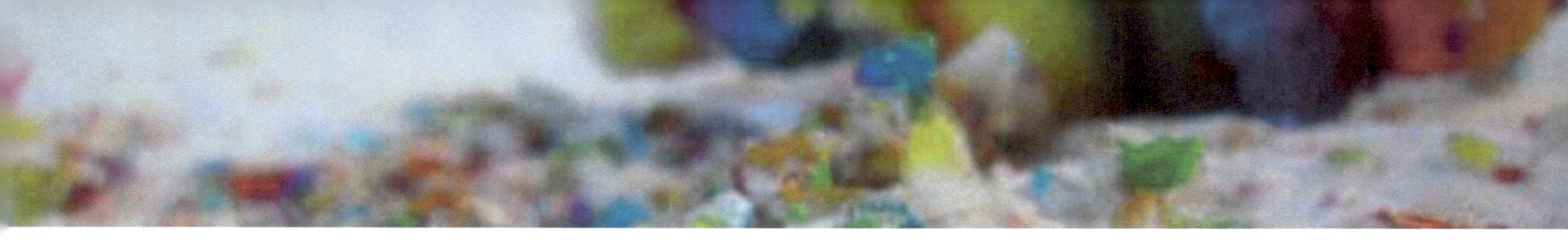

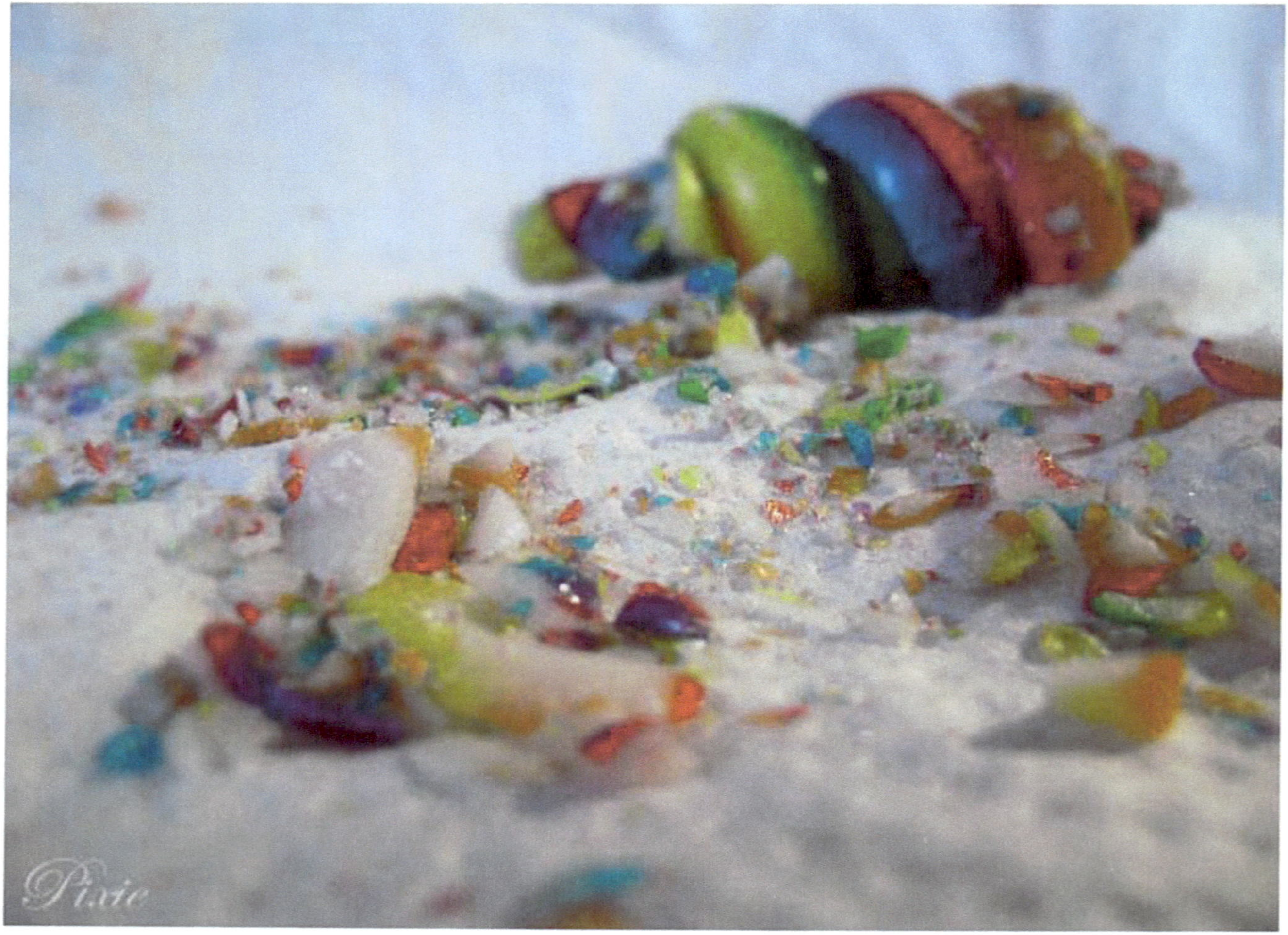

Postcard By Nancy Nunez, Student

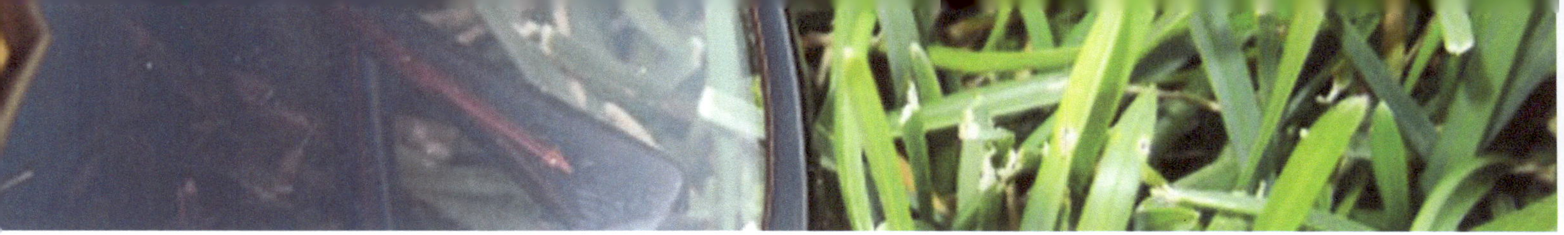

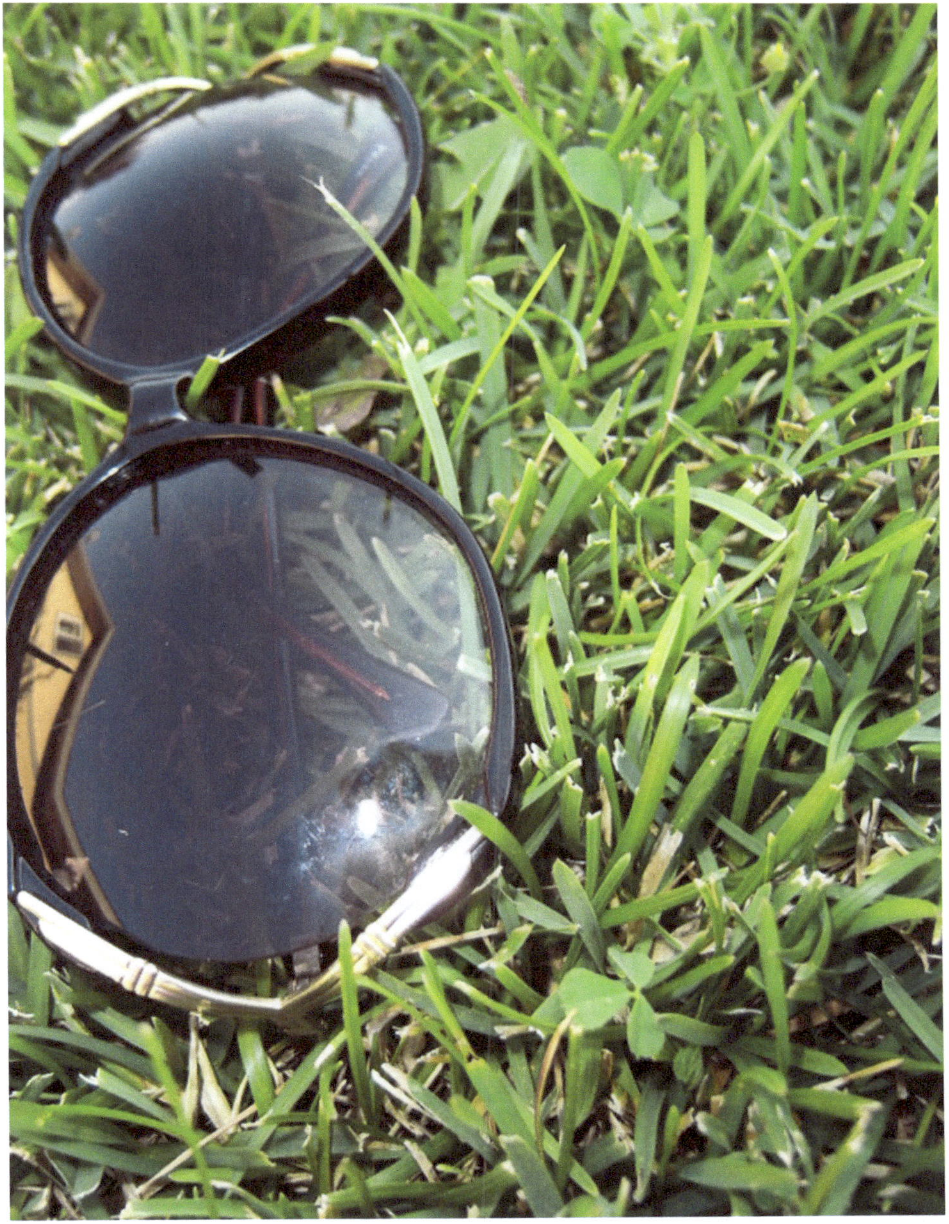

Postcard By Tricia Bohannan, Student

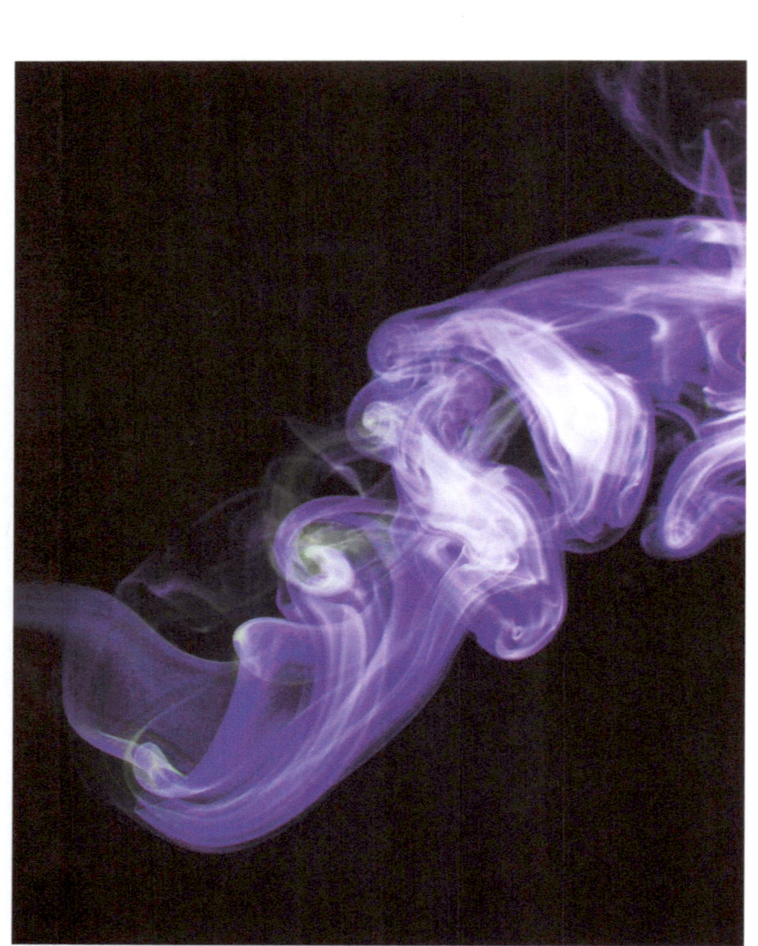

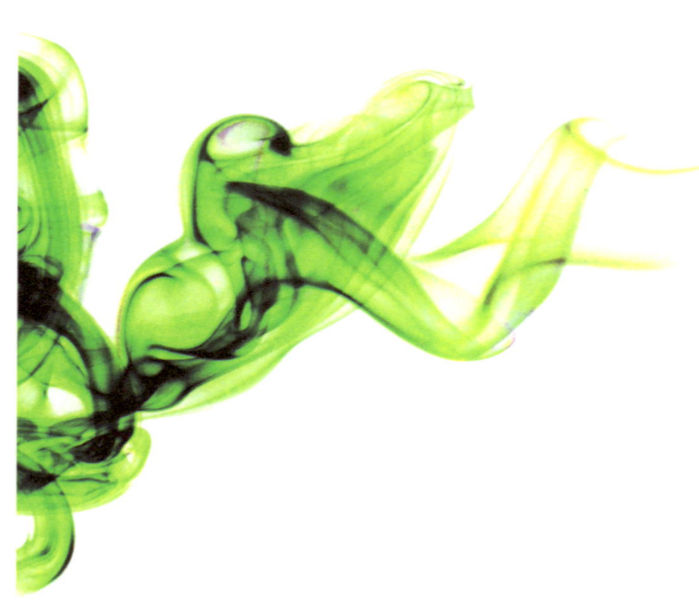

Postcards By Rebecca Humann, Student

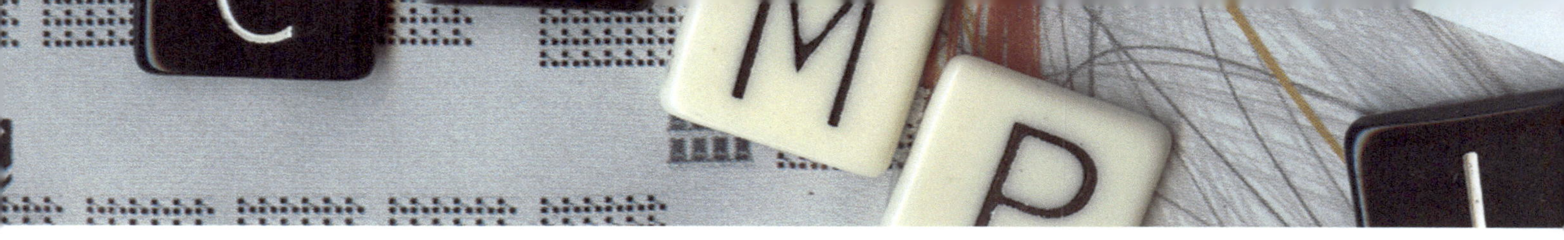

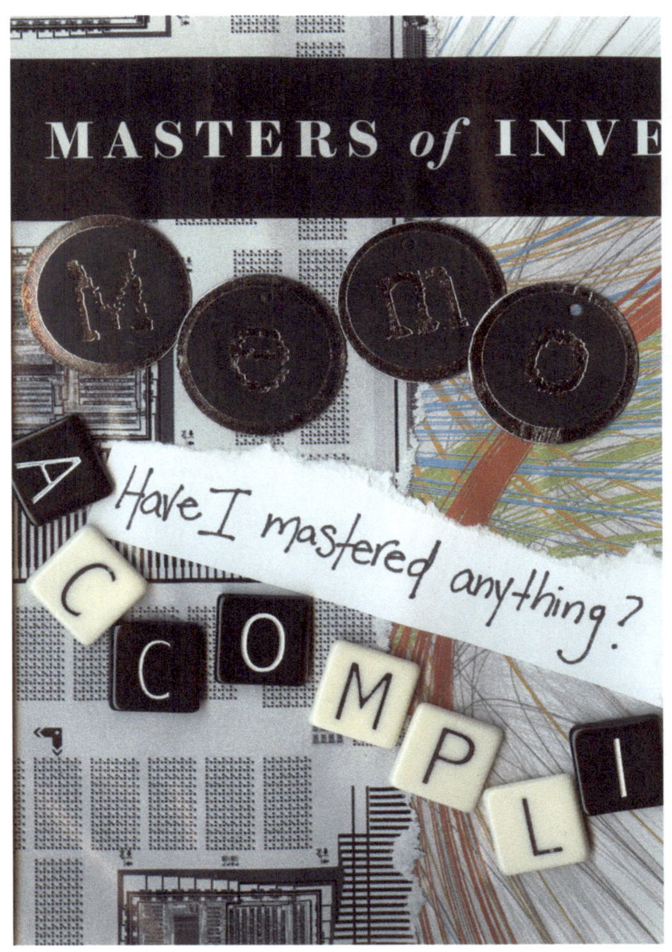

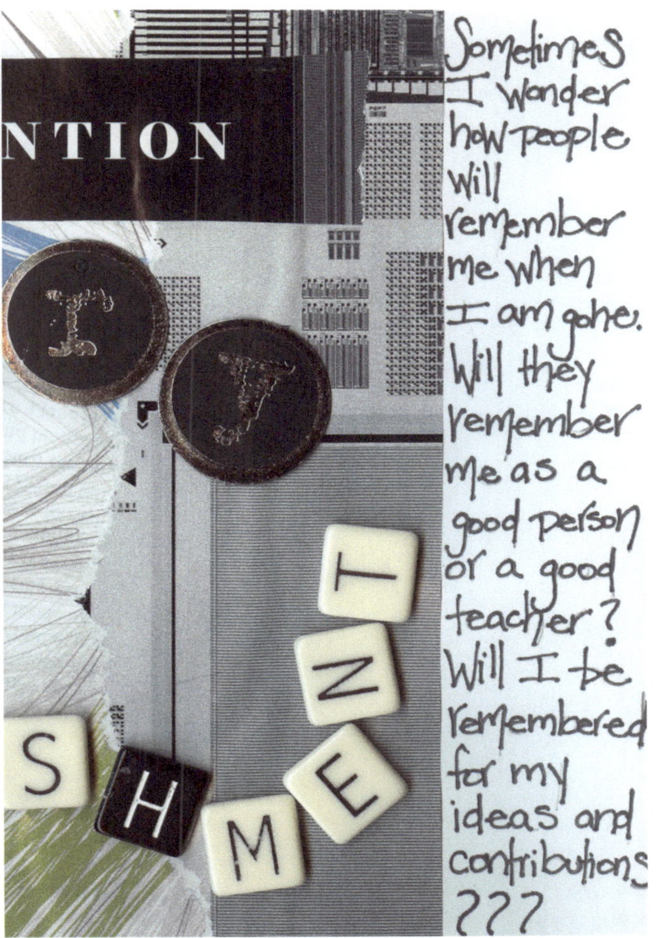

Postcards By Sarah Cress

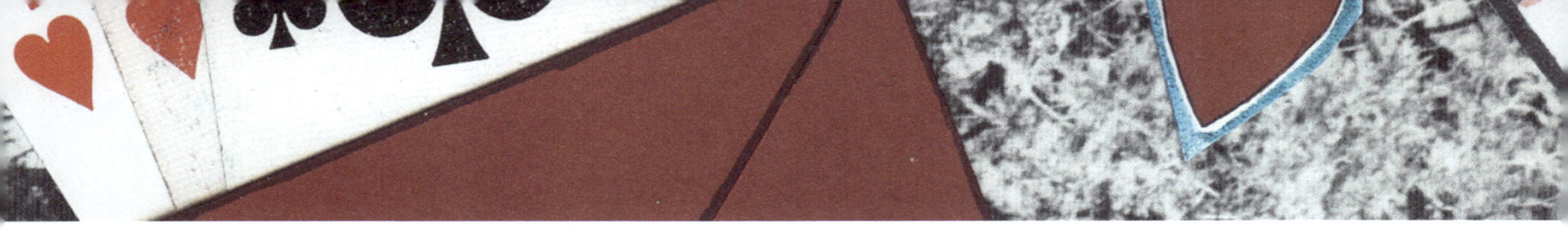

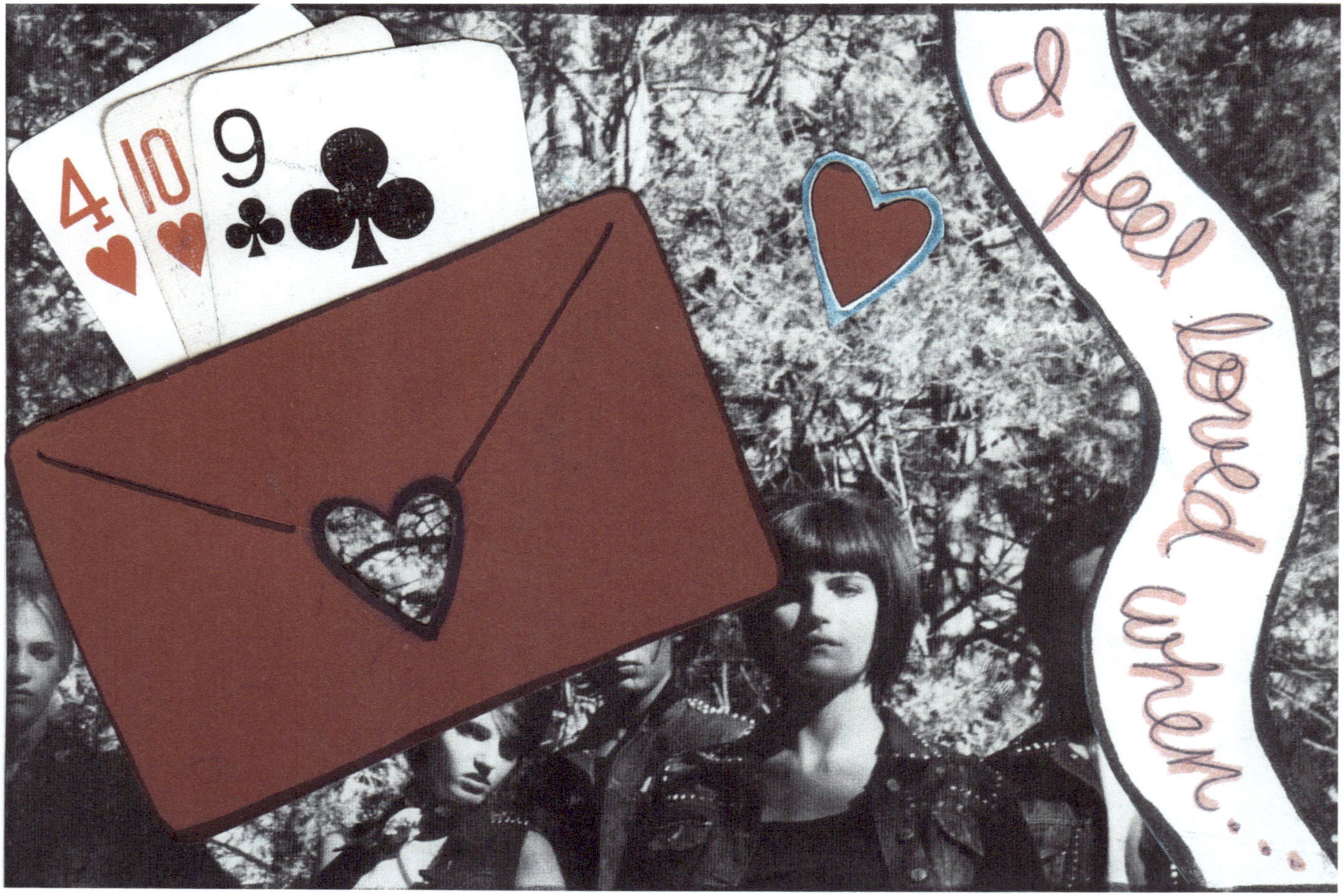

Postcard By Nicole Manning, Student

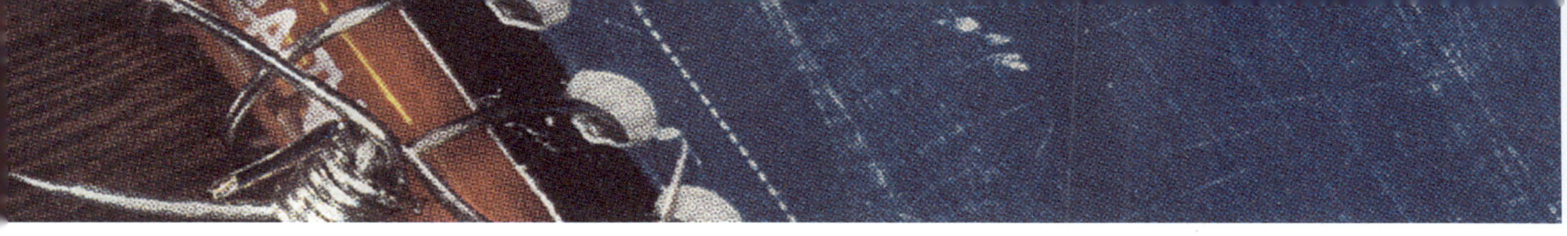

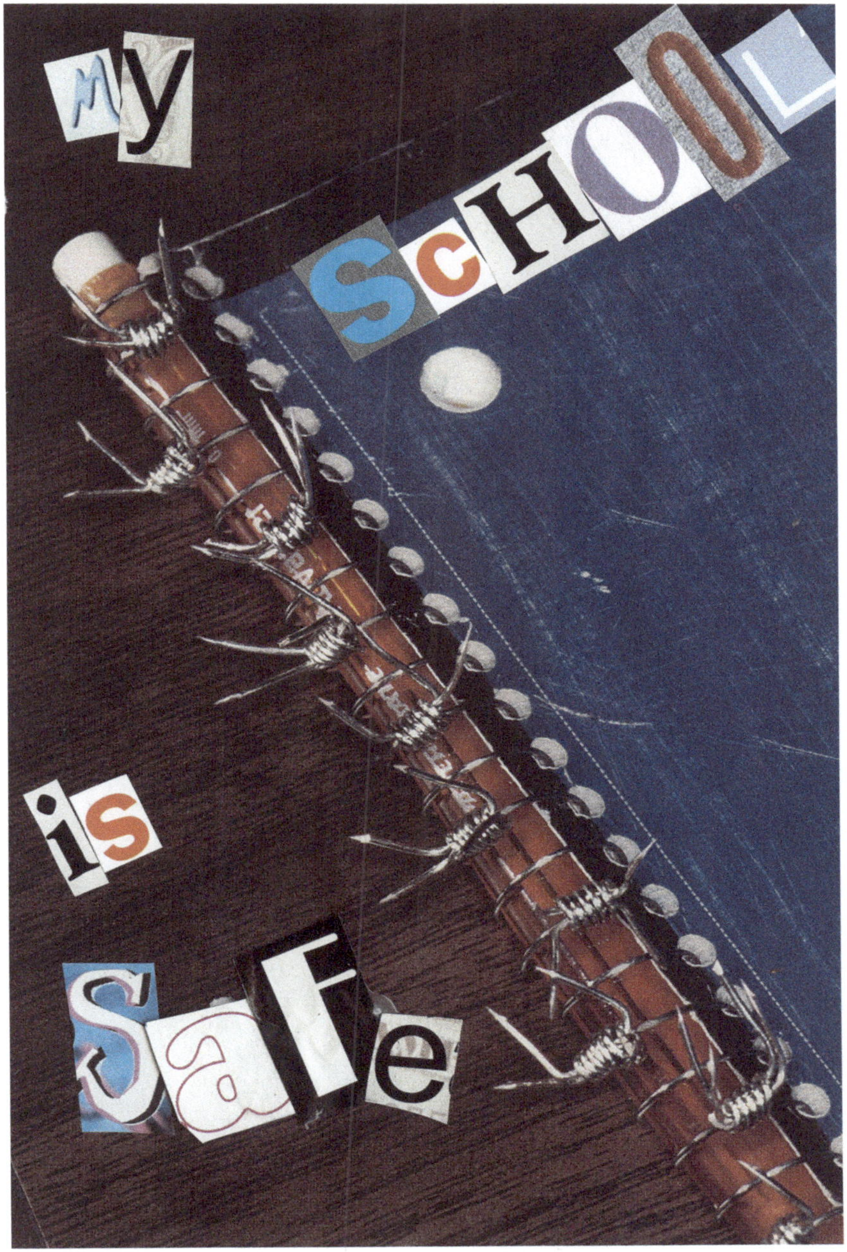

My School is Safe

*Postcard By
Zach Chacon,
Student*

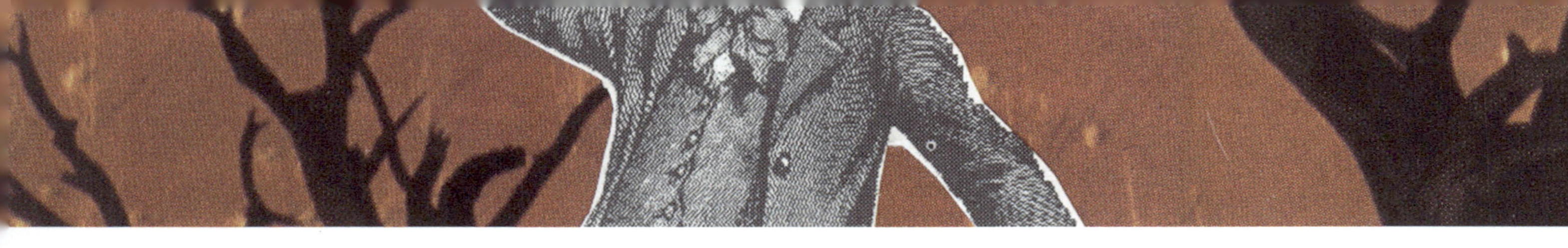

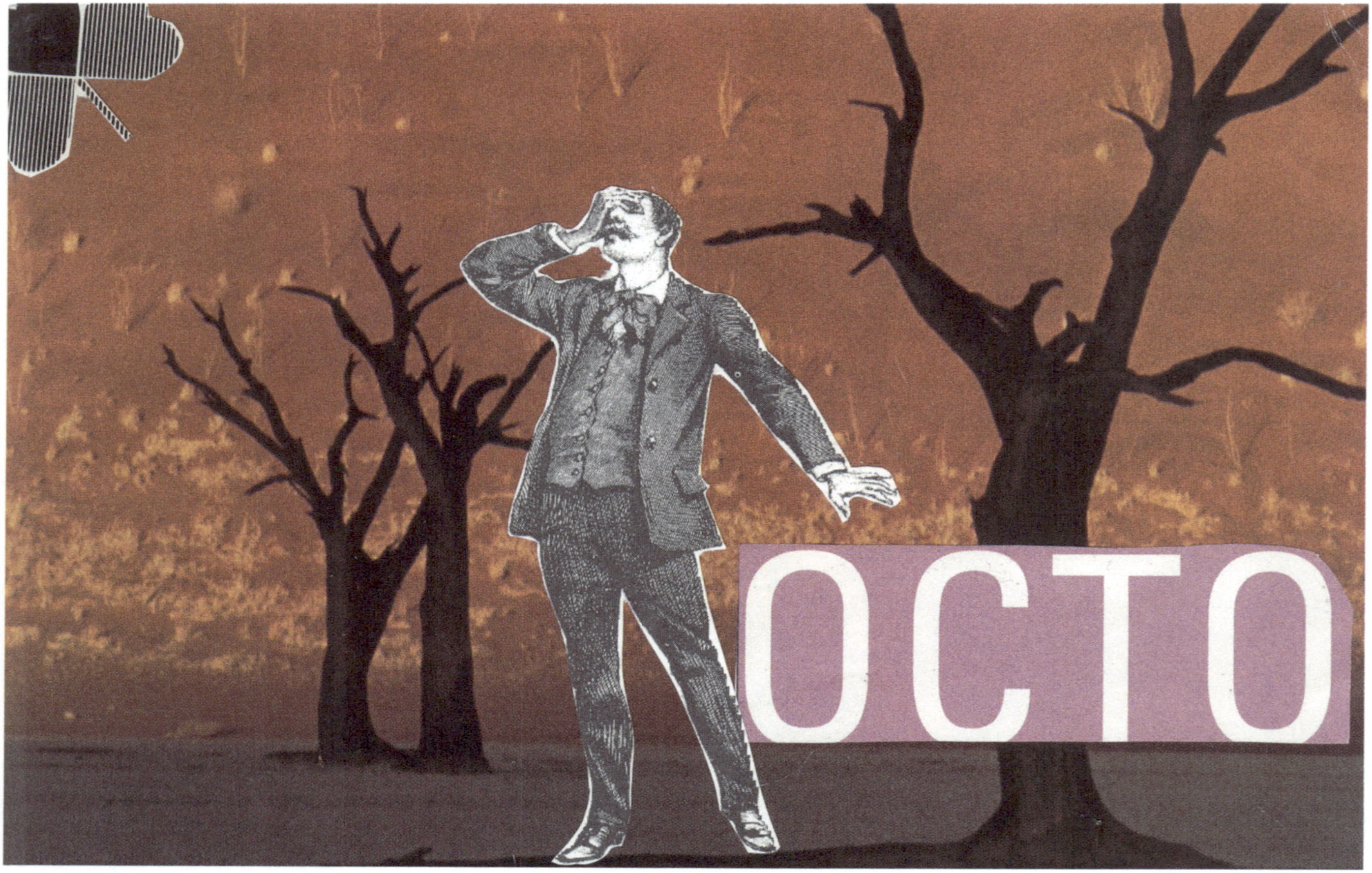

OCTO

Postcard By Tricia Bohannan, Student

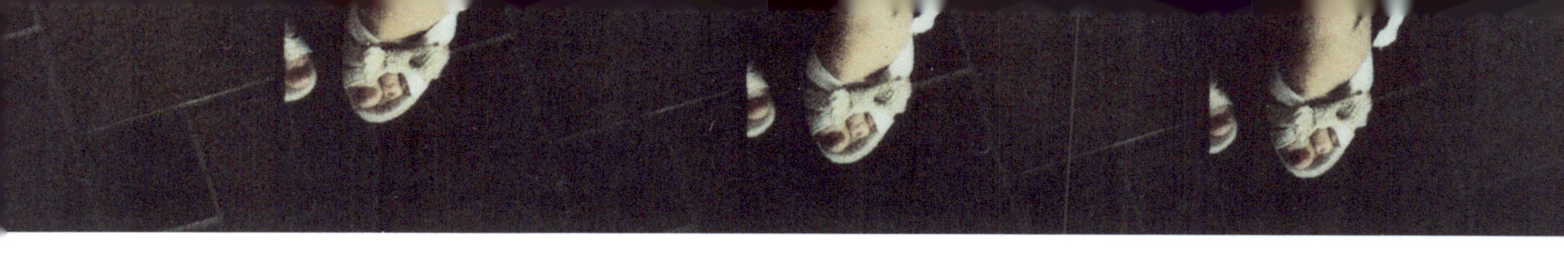

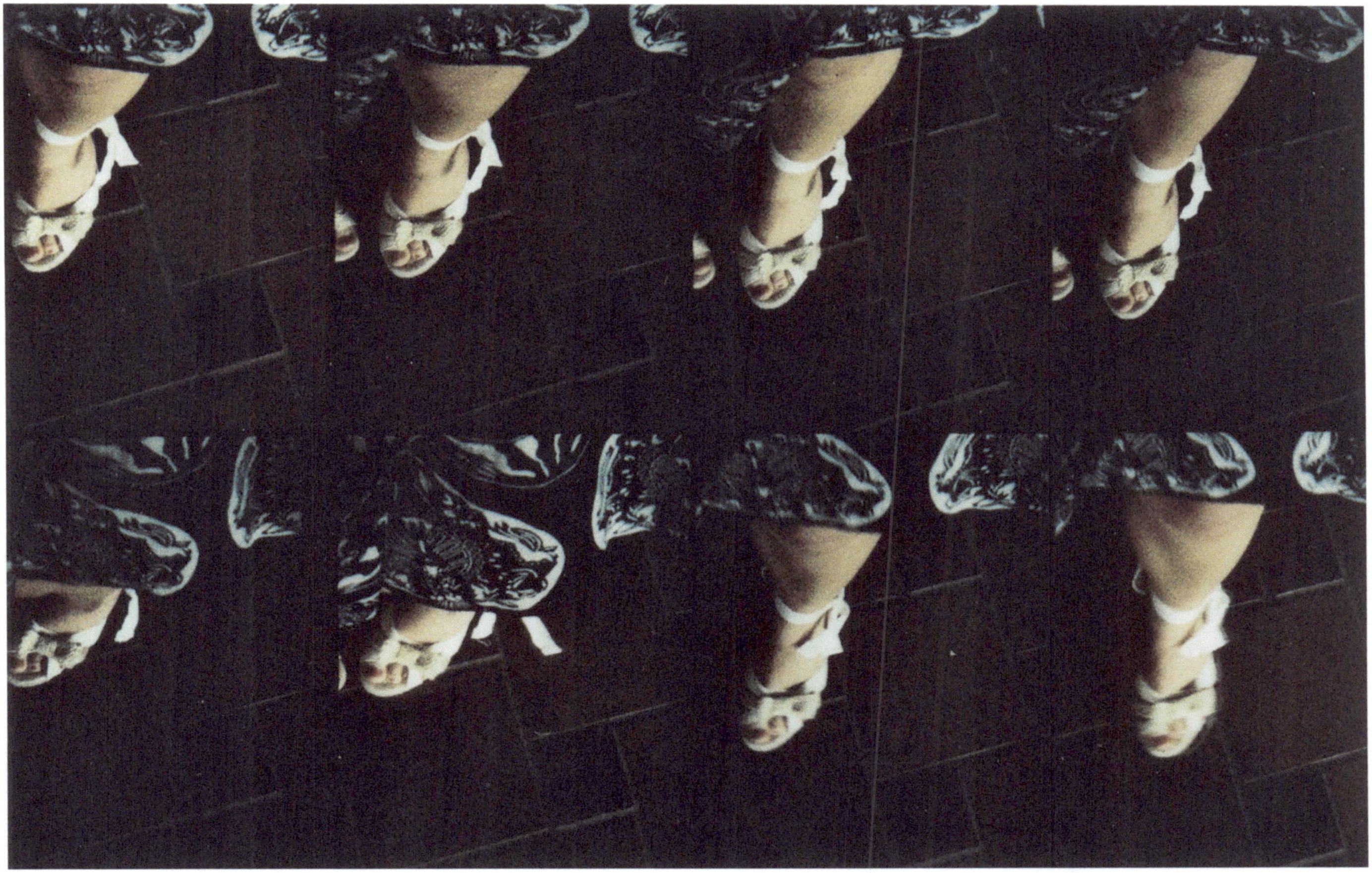

Postcard By Paige Testa, Student

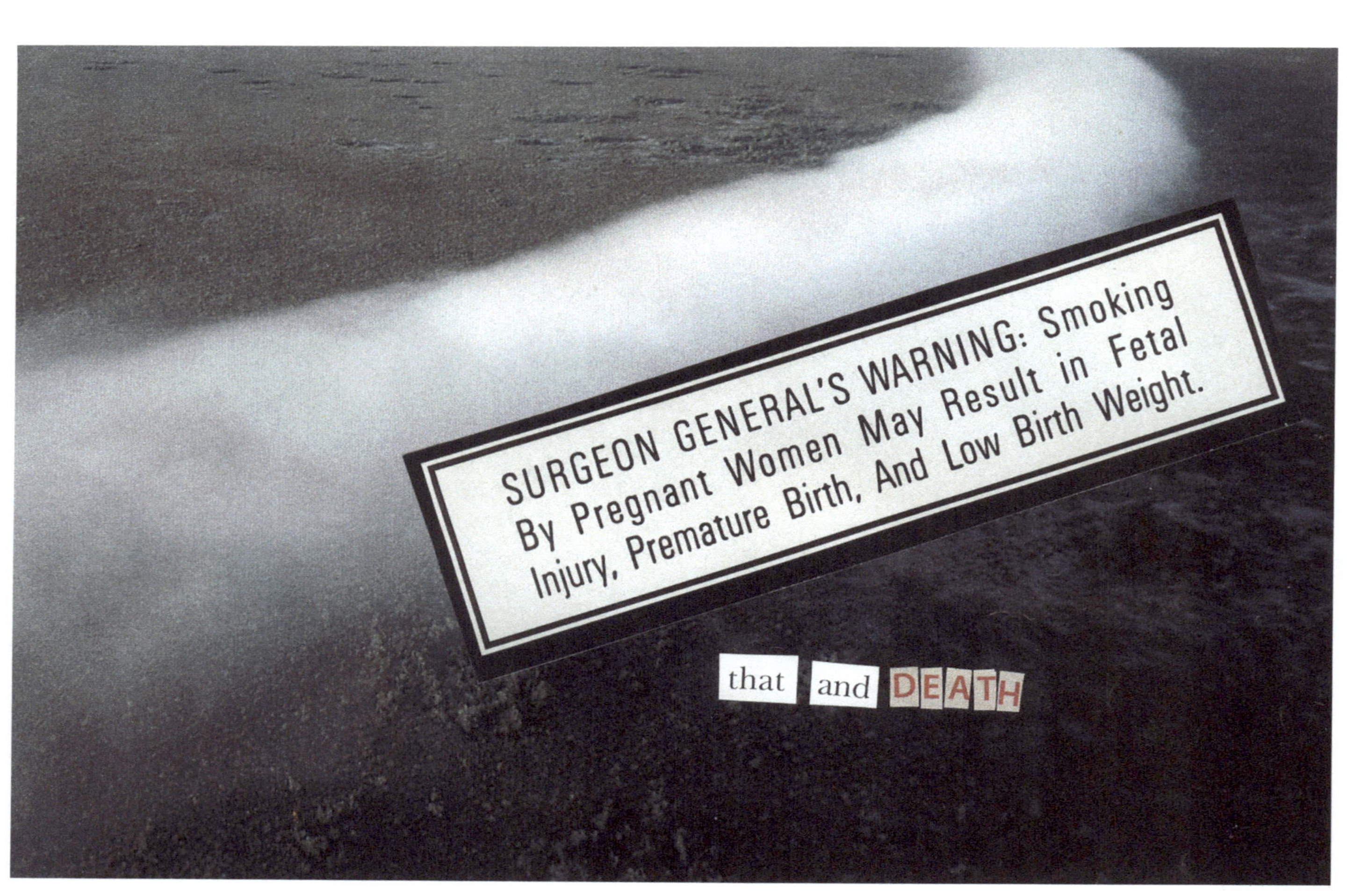

Postcard By Rebecca Humann, Student

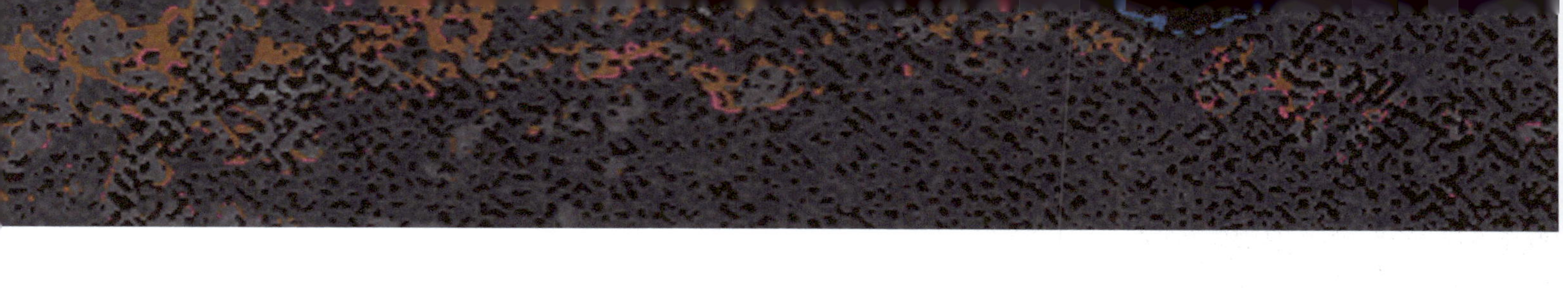

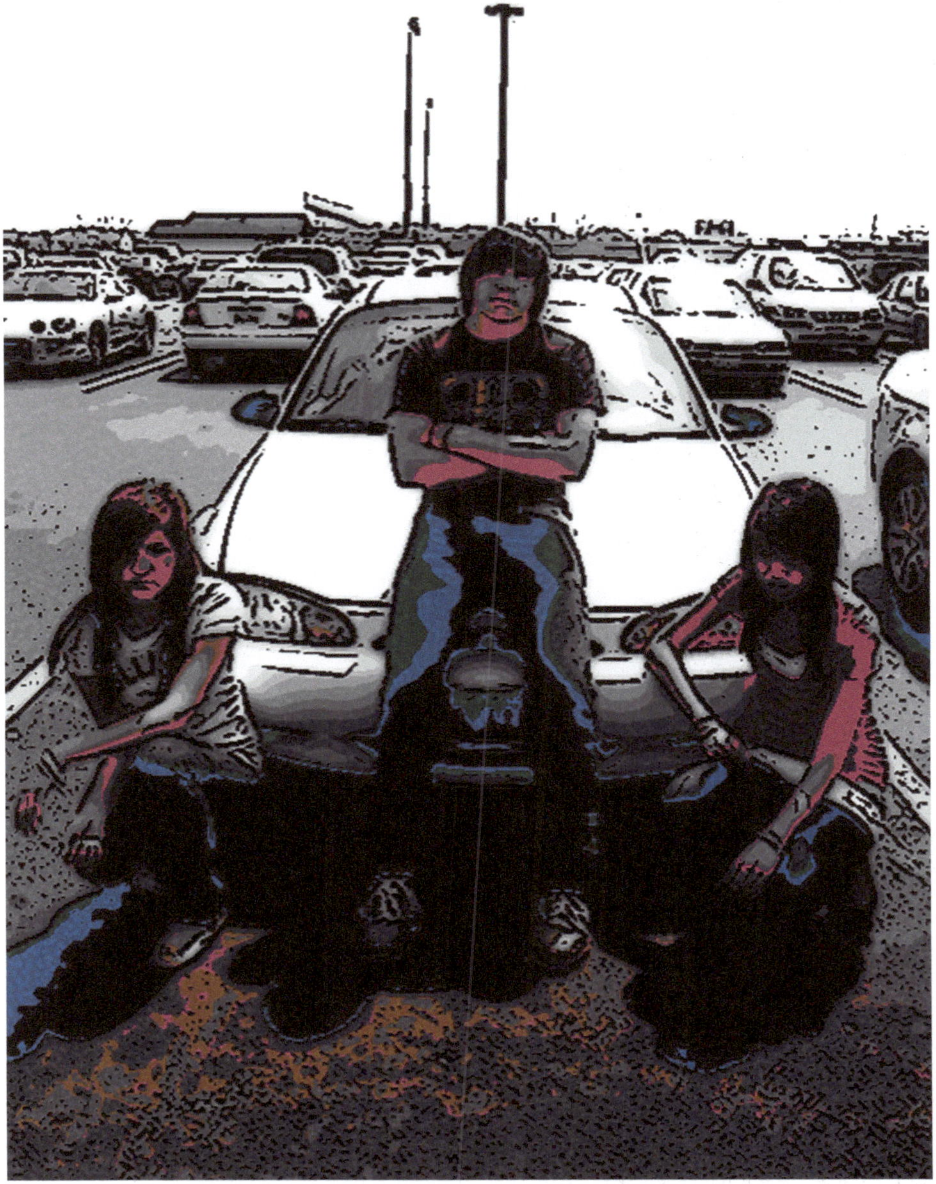

Postcard By
Jacob Brantley,
Student

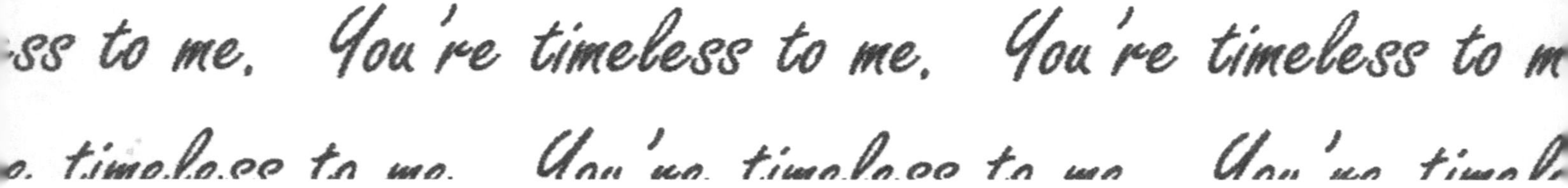

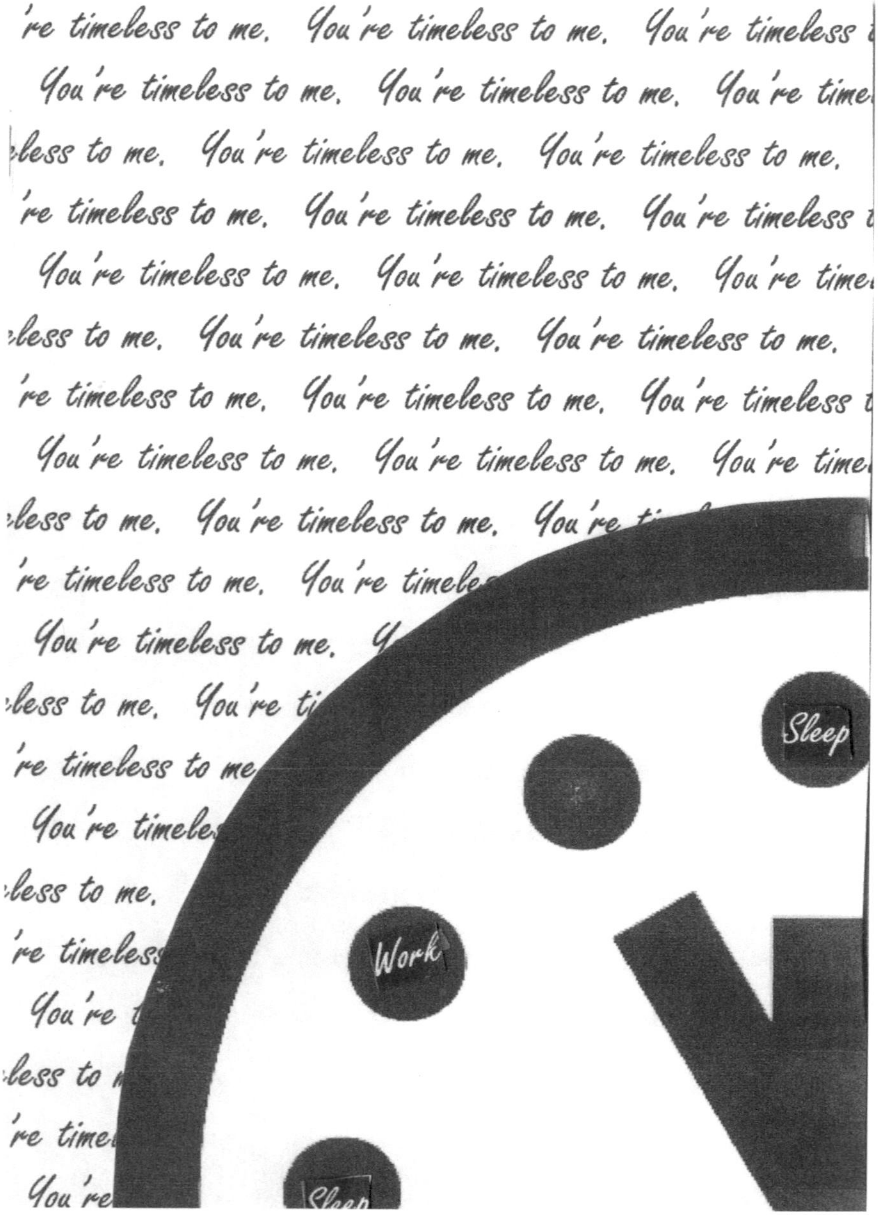

ss to me. You're timeless to me. You're timeless to m

e. timeless to me. You're timeless to me. You're timel

're timeless to me. You're timeless to me. You're timeless

You're timeless to me. You're timeless to me. You're time

less to me. You're timeless to me. You're timeless to me.

're timeless to me. You're timeless to me. You're timeless

You're timeless to me. You're timeless to me. You're time

less to me. You're timeless to me. You're timeless to me.

're timeless to me. You're timeless to me. You're timeless

You're timeless to me. You're timeless to me. You're time

less to me. You're timeless to me. You're

're timeless to me. You're timele

You're timeless to me.

less to me. You're ti

're timeless to me

You're timele

less to me.

're timeless

You're

less to

're time

You're

Sleep

Work

Sleep

Postcard By
Jennifer Left,
Student

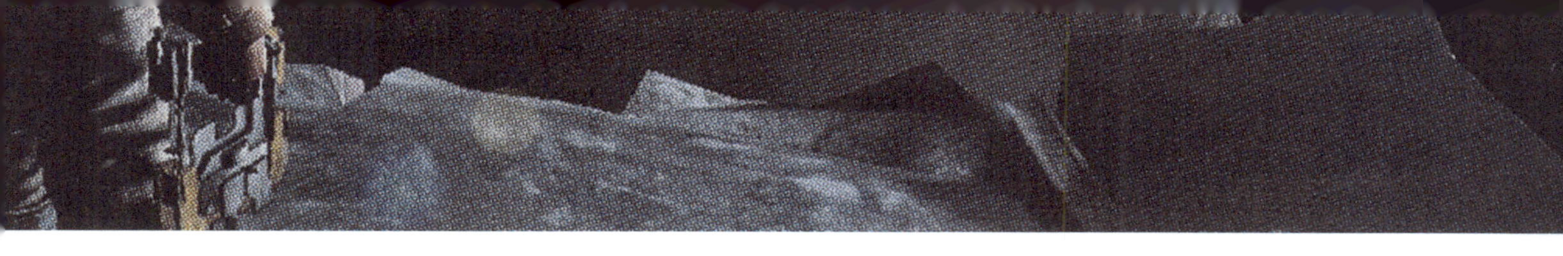

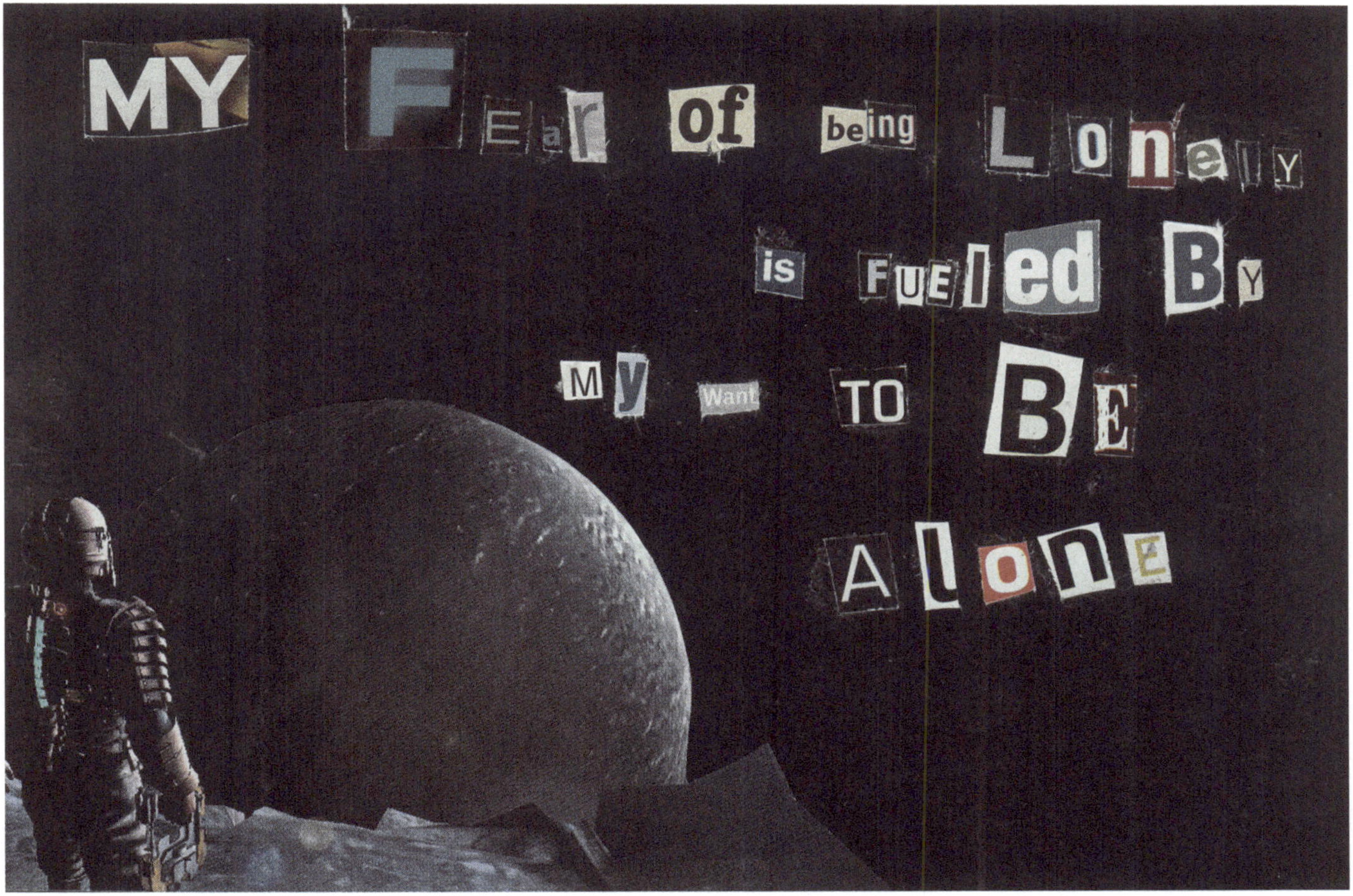

MY Fear of being Lonely
is Fueled By
My Want TO BE
Alone

Postcard By Jacob Brantley, Student

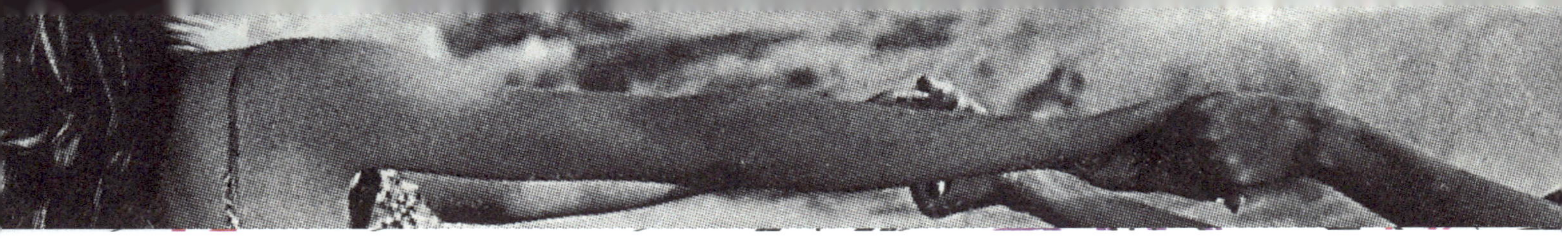

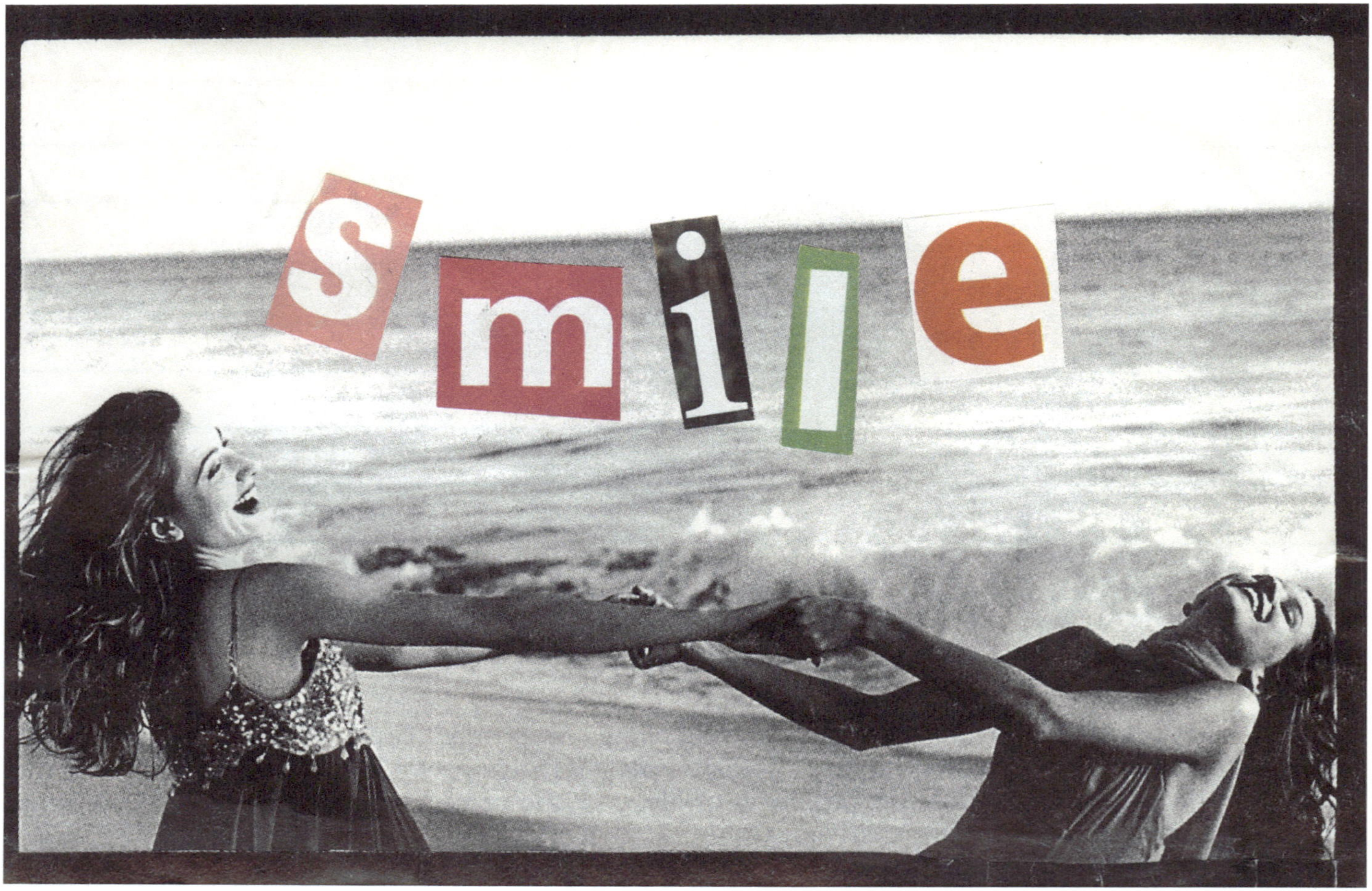

Postcard By Jennifer Left, Student

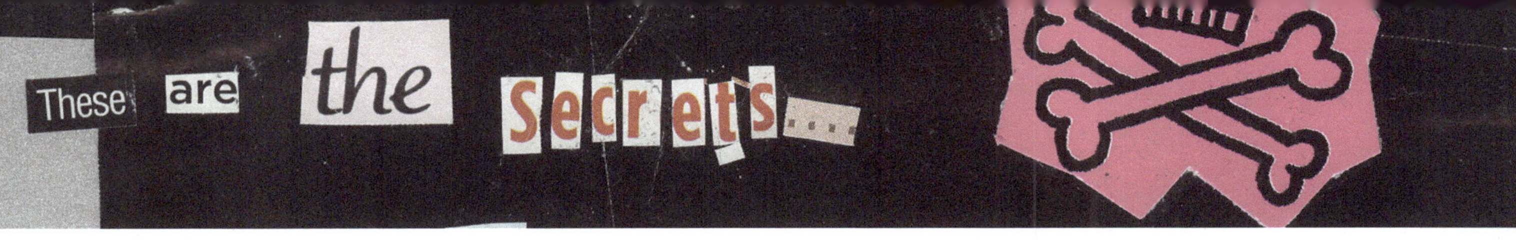

These are the Secrets....

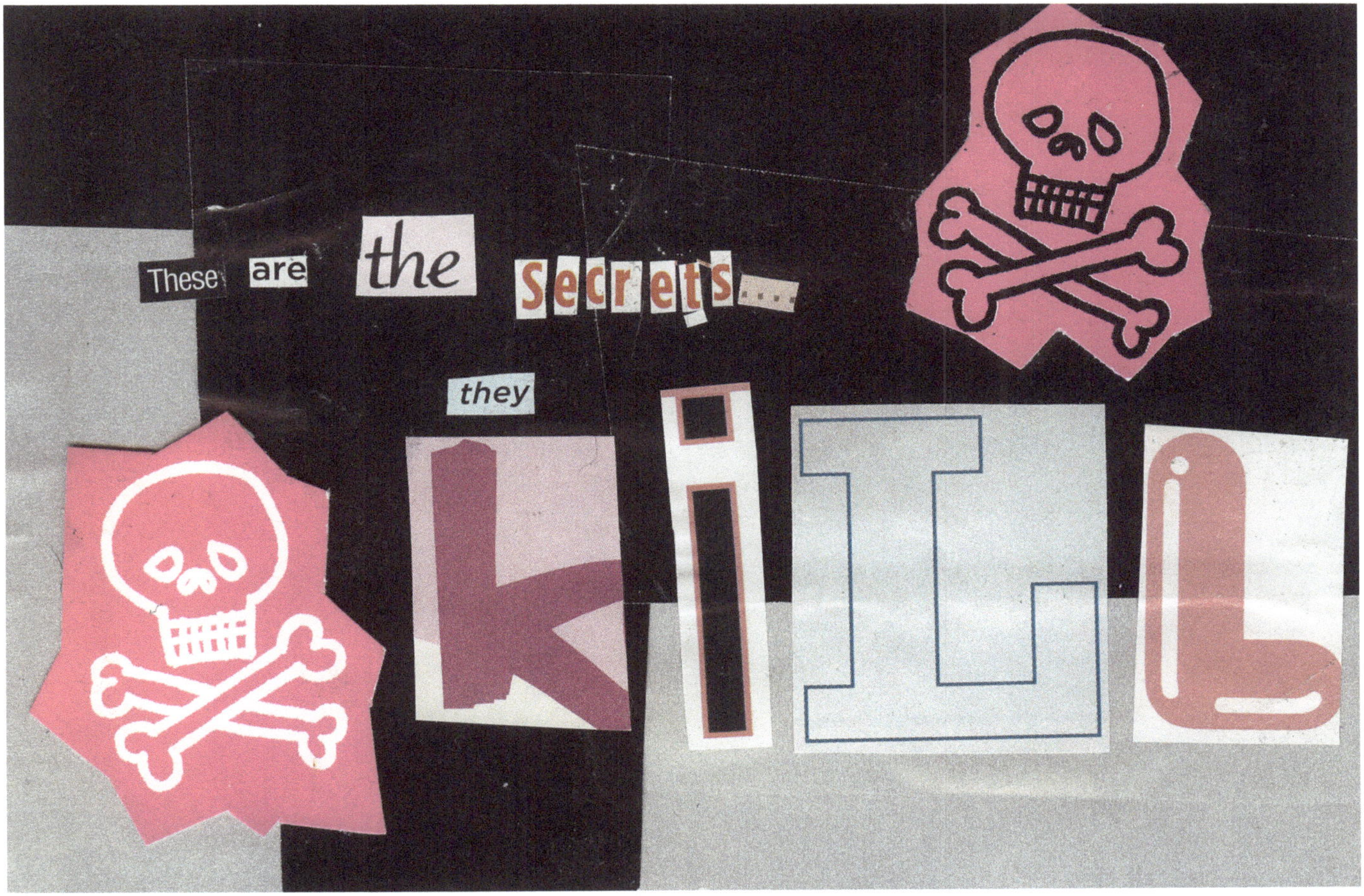

they

kill

Postcard By Rebecca Humann, Student

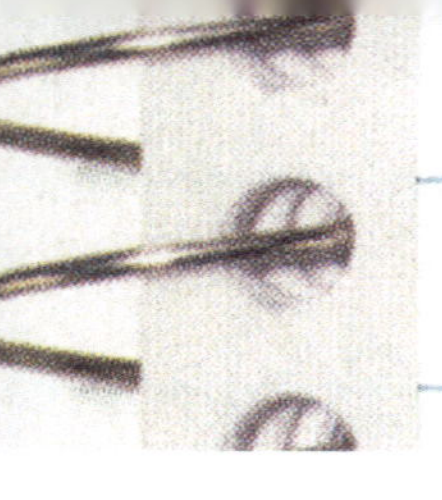

senioritis

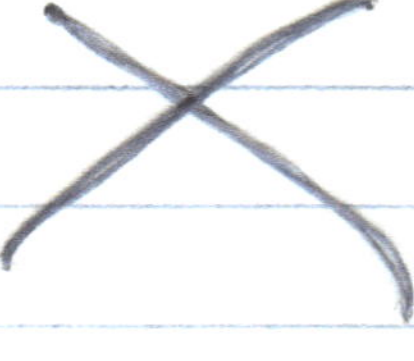

Postcard By Jennifer Left, Student

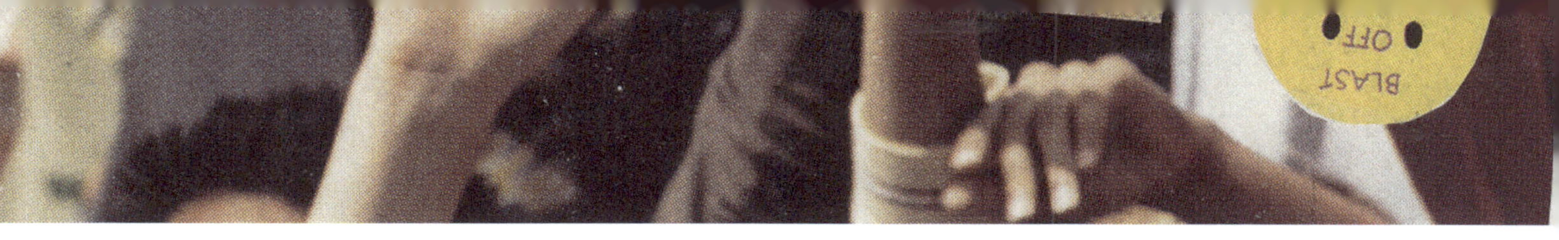

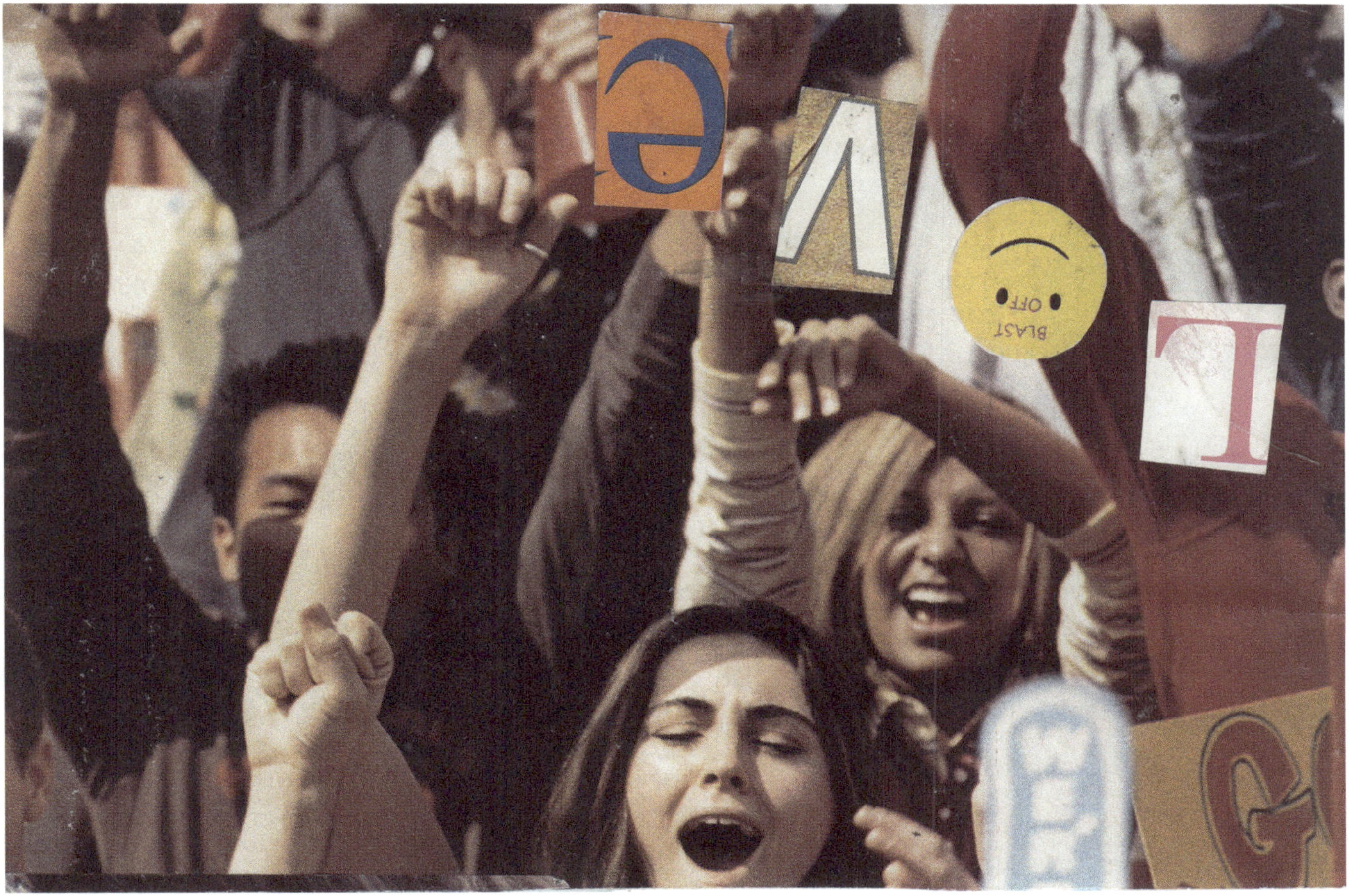

Postcard By KT Andrews, Student

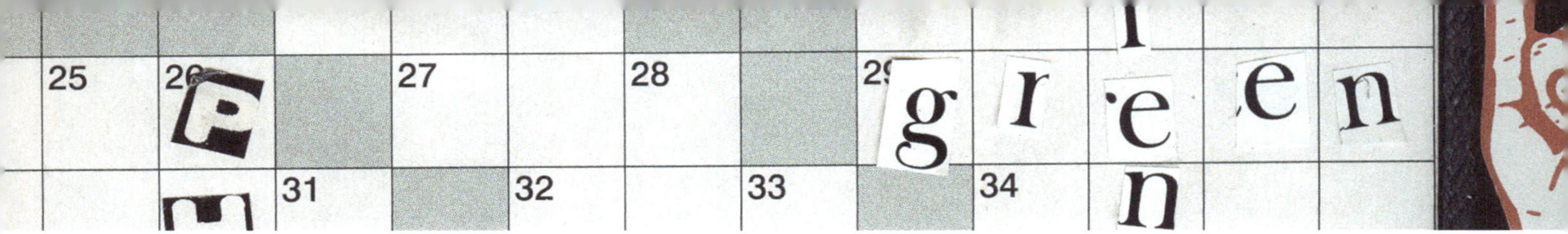

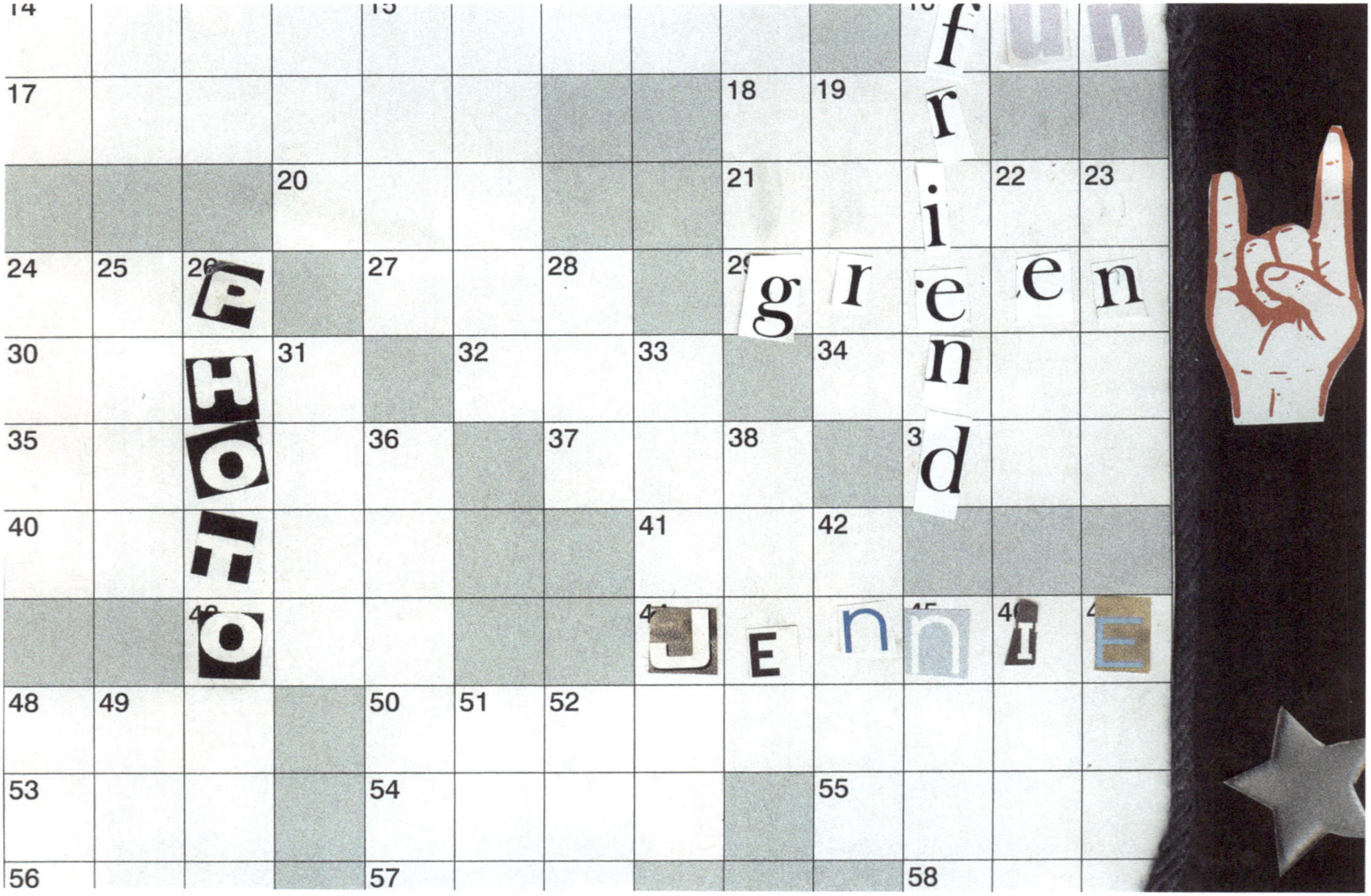

Postcard By Jennifer Left, Student

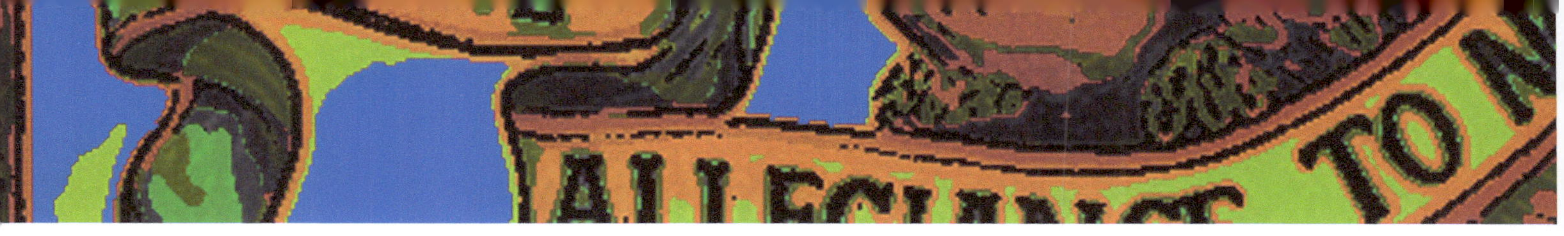

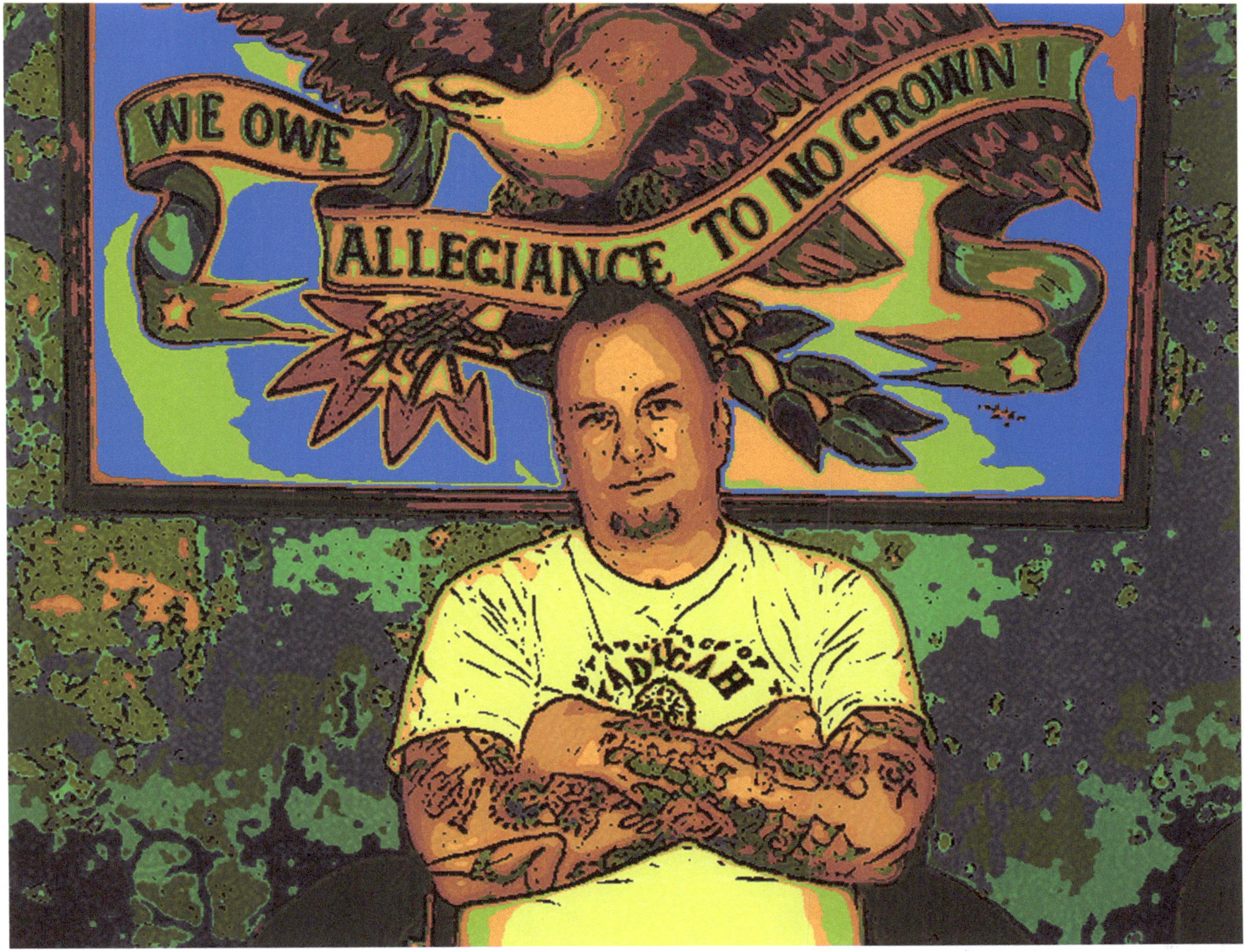

Postcard By Jacob Brantley, Student

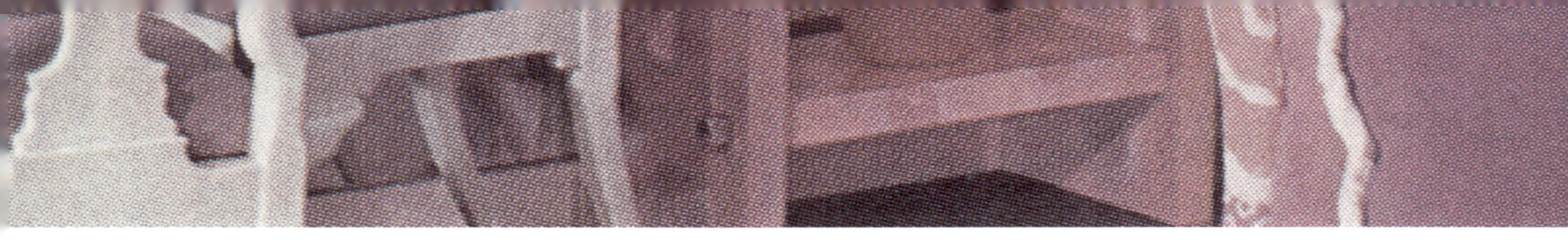

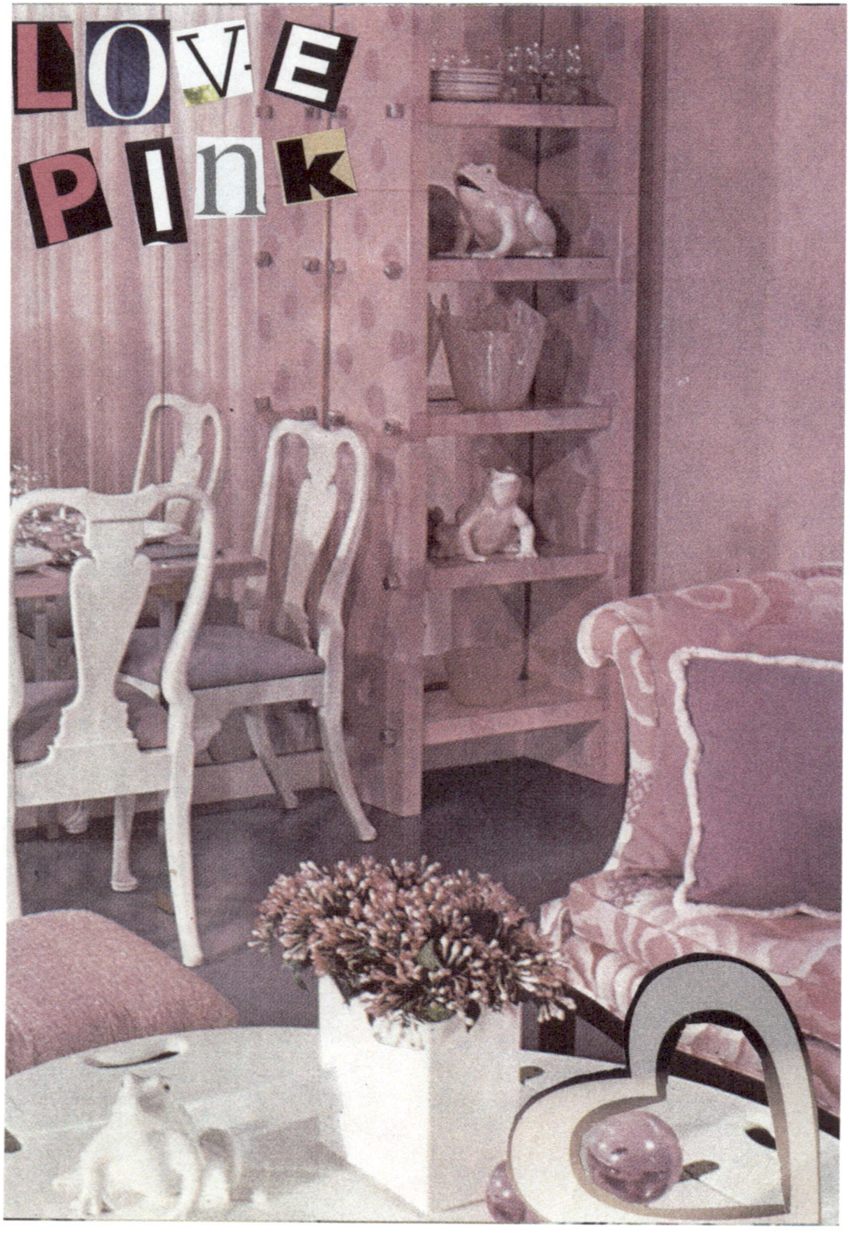

LOVE
PINK

Postcard By
Lindsey Herdrich,
Student

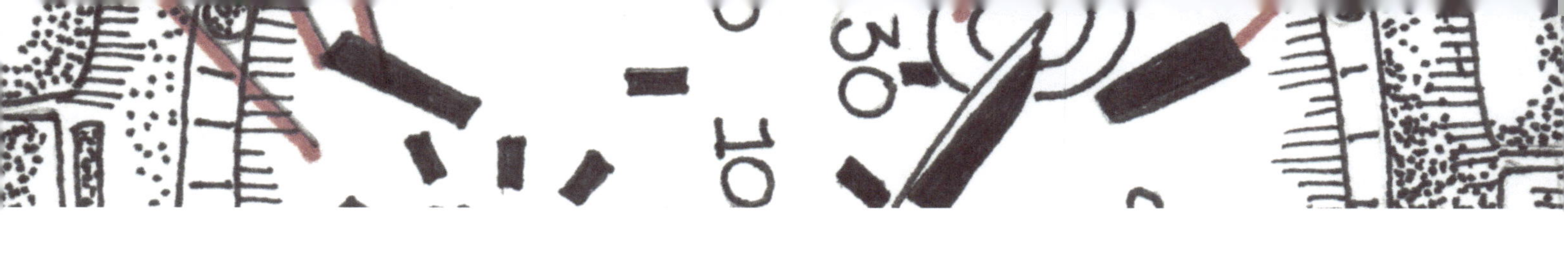

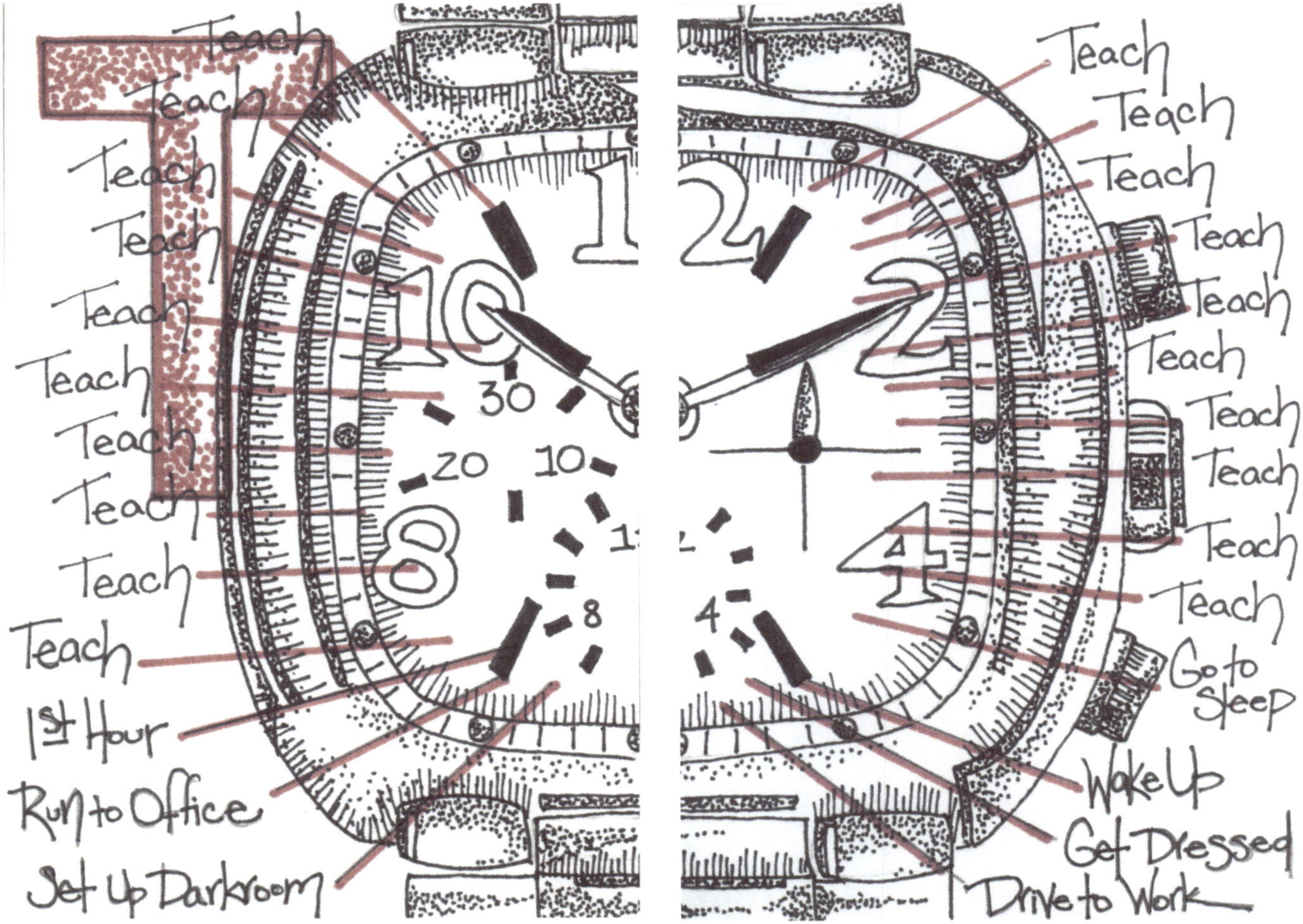

Postcards By Sarah Cress

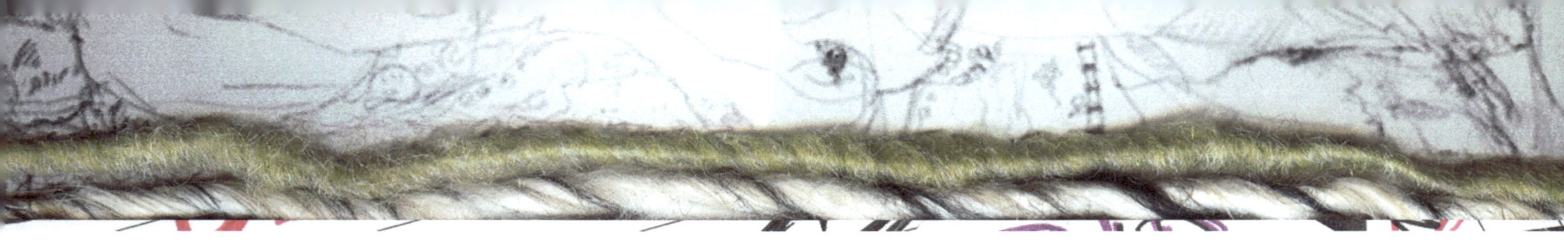

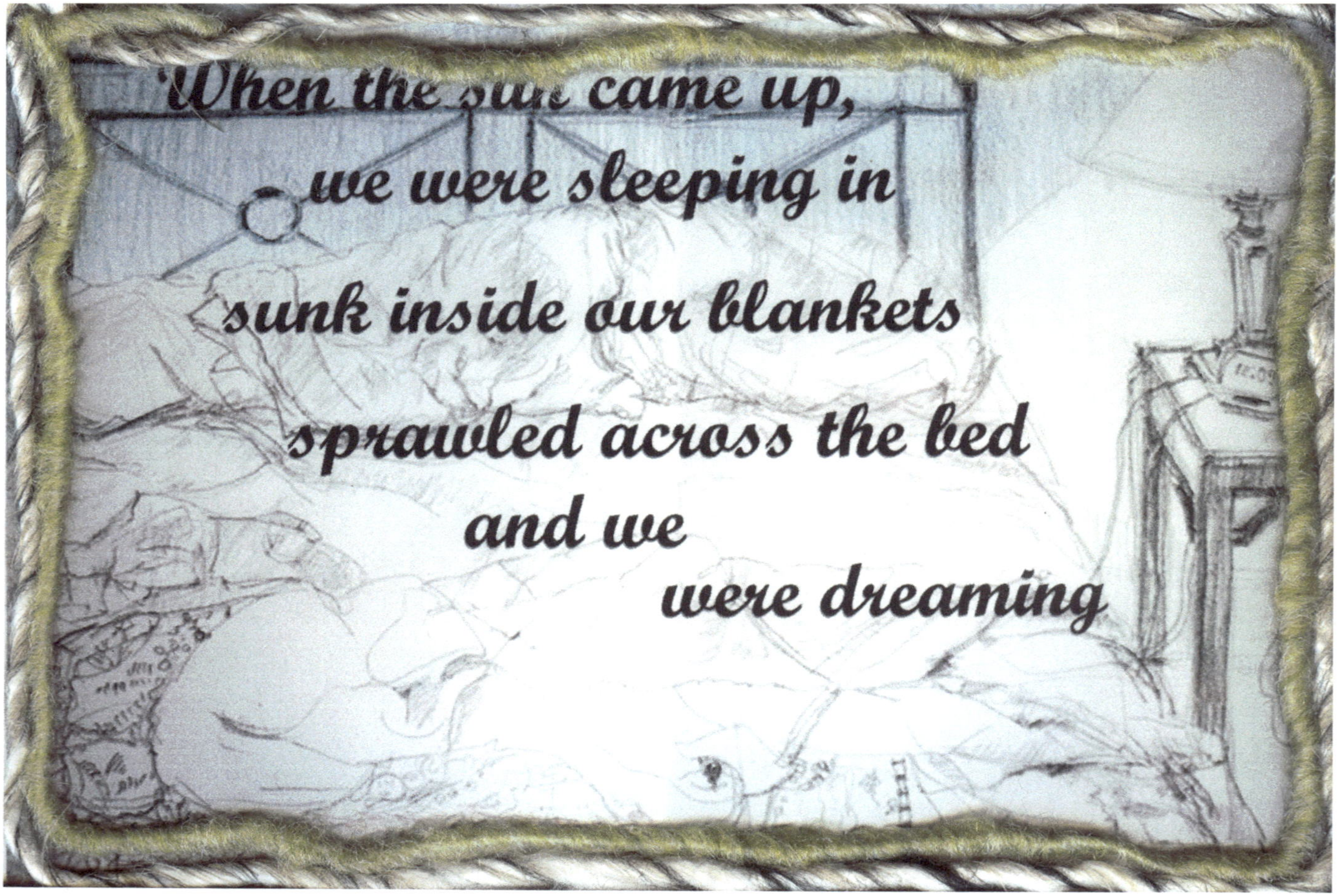

When the sun came up,
we were sleeping in
sunk inside our blankets
sprawled across the bed
and we
were dreaming

Postcard By Paige Testa, Student

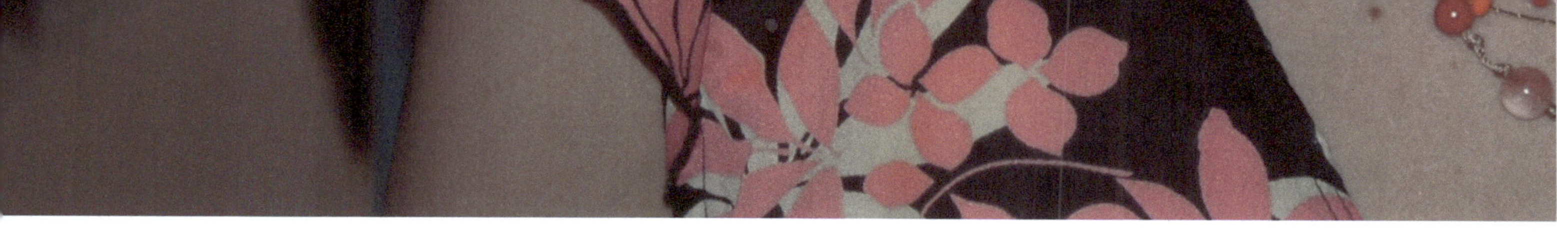

About the Author...

Sarah Nicole Cress is currently in her third year of teaching photography at Streamwood High School in Streamwood, Illinois. Sarah received her bachelor's degree in photography, her bachelor's degree in art education and her master's degree in art education from the University of Illinois at Urbana-Champaign in 2006. Although Cress' passion in the arts derives from her photography, she also enjoys various other media. This appreciation for variation is what encouraged Cress' integration of Artist Postcards in her classroom environment.

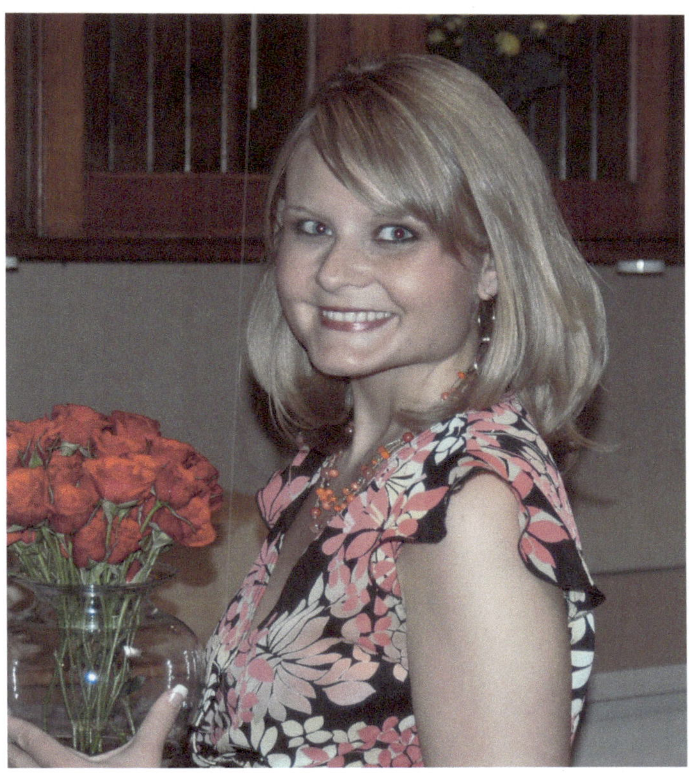

Acknowledgements...

I would like to thank my parents for their continuous guidance and encouragement. I would like to thank all of my professors at the University of Illinois at Urbana-Champaign for giving me the knowledge and confidence to do what I do best. I would like to thank Susan Gleason, a lifetime mentor and friend, for guiding me during my student teaching years and collaborating with my students and I through our Artist Postcard experience. I would like to thank my colleagues at Streamwood High School for their friendship and committment to excellence. Finally, I would like to thank my students for their amazing talent and persistence...even when they tell me my expectations are too high.

References...

Nettles, B. (1992). *Breaking the Rules: A Photo Media Cookbook*. Urbana: Inky Press Productions.

www.ingramcontent.com/pod-product-compliance
Lightning Source LLC
LaVergne TN
LVHW070142110826
845147LV00002B/306

* 9 7 8 0 5 7 8 0 2 6 2 3 7 *